KU-760-069

Pricing, Planning and Politics

A study of economic distortions
in India

SUBROTO ROY

Assistant Professor of Economics,
Virginia Polytechnic Institute and State University

Published by
THE INSTITUTE OF ECONOMIC AFFAIRS
1984

First published in May 1984

by

THE INSTITUTE OF ECONOMIC AFFAIRS

2 Lord North Street, Westminster, London SW1P 3LB

© The Institute of Economic Affairs 1984

All rights reserved

ISSN 0073-909X

ISBN 0-255 36169-6

Printed in Great Britain by

GORON PRO-PRINT CO LTD, LANCING, WEST SUSSEX

Set in Monotype Plantin 11 on 12 point

IEA PUBLICATIONS

Subscription Service

An annual subscription is the most convenient way to obtain our publications. Every title we produce in all our regular series will be sent to you immediately on publication and without further charge, representing a substantial saving.

*Subscription rates**

Britain: £15.00 p.a. including postage.

£14.00 p.a. if paid by Banker's Order.

£10.00 p.a. teachers and students who pay *personally*.

Europe and South America: £20 or equivalent.

Other countries: Rates on application. In most countries subscriptions are handled by local agents.

*These rates are *not* available to companies or to institutions.

To: The Treasurer, Institute of Economic Affairs,

2 Lord North Street,

Westminster, London SW1P 3LB.

I should like to subscribe beginning ....

I enclose a cheque/postal order for:

☐ £15.00

☐ Please send me a Banker's Order form

☐ Please send me an Invoice

☐ £10.00 [I am a teacher/student at......................................]

Name ....

Address ....

....

Signed .... Date ....

Pricing, Planning and Politics
SUBROTO ROY

1. Considerable evidence has accumulated in the last 15 years to suggest that the main policies pursued by successive governments of India since independence have been inimical to economic development.

2. Politicians and officials have failed to recognise that government has specific functions which only it can fulfil and which are essential to maintain civil peace and facilitate general prosperity.

3. Nor have they understood that prosperity flows only from innumerable individual efforts in the pursuit of private rewards.

4. An attitude of statism – the notion that government is principally responsible for improvements in the well-being of individual citizens – has pervaded public discourse throughout India.

5. The tragedy of modern India can be summed up in the truism that, when governments try to do what can be better done by the market, they neglect those functions which only government can perform.

6. The first government of independent India, under Pandit Nehru, believed that better government meant more government activity in the economy. The Indian nationalists, and especially Nehru, had just witnessed what they took to be the collapse of the market economy in the Great Depression and the rapid growth to greatness of Bolshevik Russia.

7. Nehru's socialist vision was endorsed and embellished by ostensibly 'expert' economists – whose writings revealed no understanding of prices or markets – secure in the knowledge that they were shielded from critics by the patronage of a charismatic leader.

8. India today is a maze of distorted incentives and income transfers resulting from government interference in the price system – a large and heavily-subsidised nationalised sector, labyrinthine controls over private industry, forcibly depressed agricultural prices, massive import substitution, a government monopoly of foreign-exchange transactions, an artificially over-valued currency, and extensive politicisation of the labour market.

9. Only a radical liberalisation of her economy can launch India on a path towards prosperity. Such a step appears doomed, however, by the inevitable opposition of numerous vested interests which capture the large 'rents' produced by the current controls.

10. Only the rural poor and the ordinary citizen *qua* consumer would derive an unambiguous gain from liberalisation, and neither has been or is likely to become an effective political force.

Occasional Paper 69 is published (price £1·80) by

 THE INSTITUTE OF ECONOMIC AFFAIRS
2 Lord North Street, Westminster
London SW1P 3LB   Telephone: 01-799 3745

Contents

[3]

Part III: Practice

Part IV: Reform

'The economic laws which operate in India are the same as in other countries of the world; the causes which lead to wealth among other nations lead to prosperity in India; the causes which impoverish other nations impoverish the people of India. Therefore, the line of enquiry which the economist will pursue in respect of India is the same which he adopts in inquiring into the wealth or poverty of other nations.'

> – ROMESH CHUNDER DUTT,
>   *The Economic History of India* (1906)

'Satyameva jayathey'
('Let truth be victorious')

> – Motto of the Indian Republic

Preface

IEA *Occasional Papers* are designed, *inter alia*, to present to students and teachers of economics, and to laymen interested in economic thinking, material originally delivered or published for specialist groups of listeners or readers. They are also used to present material that does not easily fall within the *Hobart Papers*, *Hobart Paperbacks* or other IEA series.

In 1971, the IEA published a *Research Monograph* (No. 27) entitled *India: Progress or Poverty?*, by the Indian economist Sudha Shenoy, which documented the historical origins and detrimental consequences of India's espousal of wholesale economic planning. Thirteen years later, in Occasional Paper 69, another Indian economist returns to the subject to show that the system of stultifying controls which Miss Shenoy so emphatically condemned for imprisoning India in poverty is still very much in place. In the intervening period, economic policy-making in India has continued to perpetuate poverty and retard progress.

Dr Subroto Roy's critique in this *Occasional Paper* draws on the teaching of a variety of schools of economic thought, as well as benefiting from some original insights of his own. Two of those schools – one comparatively old and one comparatively new – have attracted increasing attention in recent years. The so-called Austrian School, dating back to a group of late 19th-century economists at the University of Vienna (of which the leading lights were Carl Menger, Friedrich von Wieser and Eugen von Böhm-Bawerk), has recaptured the interest of scholars largely because of the towering influence today of F. A. Hayek, whose voluminous writings have developed and refined Austrian teaching.[1] Central to Austrian

---

[1] Extracts from a number of Professor Hayek's works are assembled in *A Tiger by the Tail: The Keynesian legacy of inflation*, compiled and introduced by Sudha R. Shenoy, Hobart Paperback No. 4, IEA, 1972, 2nd edn. 1978.

analysis is an emphasis on individual price changes as indispensable sources of empirical information not obtainable from other sources or by other means. It is in marked contrast with other schools which concentrate on macro-economic aggregates and neglect the market processes which determine *relative* prices. In a world pervaded by uncertainty, circumstances are continually changing and knowledge of those changes is first acquired by the individuals most directly concerned. As they adapt their actions to the changed circumstances, they alter the prices and/or other elements in the data – to which other individuals adapt their actions, and so on. The market process can thus use more of the data available to individuals more effectively than can other methods which attempt to co-ordinate individual actions. Decentralised decision-making through markets is vastly more efficient than the 'grand plan'.

The second, comparatively new, school of thought is the theory of public choice (known also as the economics of politics or bureaucracy). Developed in the USA primarily by Professors James Buchanan and Gordon Tullock, public choice applies economic theory and analysis to political decision-making.[1] Specifically, it jettisons the conventional assumption of standard economic theory that, whereas private behaviour in the market is motivated by self-interest, politicians and bureaucrats are motivated solely by a desire to pursue the general public interest. In short, it posits a *political* market in which the actors seek to maximise their *own* net benefits, whether of a pecuniary or non-pecuniary nature.

Dr Roy explains how India's centralised system of economic planning has produced a maze of distorted incentives and income transfers. That system, he says, is the product of India's long-standing submission to statist thinking – to the belief that government is the fount of individual well-being, reinforced in more modern times by the notion that government is the engine of economic growth and development. Statist thinking spread, if anything, under British rule; but it was in newly-independent India that it was elevated to official ideology in Pandit Nehru's 'socialist vision'. That vision, Dr Roy notes scornfully, was buttressed and adorned by ostensibly 'expert' economists – whose writings, however,

[1] For an introduction to public choice theory, Gordon Tullock, *The Vote Motive*, Hobart Paperback No. 9, IEA, 1976, and James M. Buchanan *et al.*, *The Economics of Politics*, IEA Readings No. 18, IEA, 1978.

revealed no understanding of prices or markets – content to bask in the approbation of a charismatic leader.

Dr Roy examines at length the economic consequences of the collectivist apparatus constructed in India – the large and heavily-subsidised nationalised sector, the labyrinthine controls over private enterprise, forcibly depressed agricultural prices, massive import substitution, the government monopoly of foreign-exchange transactions, the artificially over-valued currency, and the extensive politicisation of the labour market. He pinpoints the distortions and inefficiencies they have produced – not to mention the corruption. And, most striking of all, he exposes the absurdities: that, because government does not usually allow a firm to expand – regardless of its efficiency – if there is excess capacity in its industry, high-cost firms can count on staying in business simply by maintaining significant excess capacity; that exports of 'new', non-traditional manufactures like engineering goods are subsidised while exports of goods in which India has traditionally enjoyed a comparative advantage are taxed and even sometimes banned; that, because capital-intensive goods are India's main imports and labour-intensive goods its main exports, an over-valued rupee distorts prices in a way which en-courages capital-intensive production processes – in a country with a demonstrable abundance of relatively inexpensive labour; and so on.

Not the least damaging distortion has been the discrimination in favour of industry against agriculture and in favour of the urban against the rural poor – a policy which has stimulated large-scale migration from the land to swell the urban unemployed. The World Bank has in recent years taken to enjoining developing countries to 'get the prices right' as the single most effective policy for economic growth. Very few countries would stand to benefit more from heeding that advice than India.

Dr Roy ends by proposing a 'tentative manifesto' of reforms to liberalise the Indian economy which, he says, are essential if India is ever to be launched on a path to general prosperity. He is, however, pessimistic about their prospects of being implemented, for reasons he derives from public choice analysis. In brief, there are too many vested interests in the *status quo* of corruption and controls to permit it to be dismantled. Economic life is so politi-cised, and 'rent-seeking' so remunerative to many groups in society, that it is well-nigh impossible to envisage sufficiently widespread and powerful support for radical reform. Even private industry as a whole would probably resist reform, for it has already traded its freedom for the comfortable protection of import barriers against foreign competition. Only the rural poor and the ordinary consumer *qua* consumer would derive an unambiguous gain from liberalisation of the economy, and neither, Dr Roy sadly concludes, has been or is likely to become an effective political force.

Although the constitution of the Institute obliges it to dissociate its Trustees, Directors and Advisers from the author's analysis and conclusions, it offers Dr Roy's *Occasional Paper* as an informed and incisive case study of an economy which is an object lesson to the world's poorer countries in how *not* to develop.

January 1984 MARTIN WASSELL

The Author

SUBROTO ROY was born in 1955 and was educated at St Paul's School, Darjeeling, and Haileybury College, Hertford. He graduated from the London School of Economics in 1976 with First Class Honours in mathematical economics and econometrics. He received his Ph.D. from the University of Cambridge in 1982 for a dissertation entitled 'On liberty and economic growth: preface to a philosophy for India'.

Dr Roy has been a research scholar of Corpus Christi College, Cambridge, a visitor at the Indian Statistical Institute, New Delhi, the Delhi School of Economics, the Centre for Study of Public Choice at Virginia Polytechnic Institute and State University, and the Department of Economics at Cornell University. He is currently assistant professor of economics at Virginia Polytechnic Institute and State University.

Pricing, Planning and Politics
SUBROTO ROY

1. INTRODUCTION

IN THE last 15 years, considerable evidence has accumulated to suggest that the most important policies pursued by successive governments of independent India have not been conducive to economic development, and have indeed gone against some of the most basic lessons that political economy has to offer. Fore-warnings of the present predicament of India had come from a few economists in the late 1950s and early 1960s, but their arguments were either ignored or maligned as dogmatic and motivated by 'ideology'.[1] My thesis in this *Occasional Paper* will be that,

---

[1] The early studies notably include: B. R. Shenoy, 'A note of dissent', *Papers relating to the formulation of the Second Five-Year Plan*, Government of India Planning Commission, Delhi, 1955; *Indian Planning and Economic Development*, Asia Publishing, Bombay, 1963, especially pp. 17-53; P. T. Bauer, *Indian Economic Policy and Development*, George Allen & Unwin, London, 1961; M. Friedman, unpublished memorandum to the Government of India, November 1955 (referred to in Bauer, *op. cit.*, p. 59 ff.); and, some years later, Sudha Shenoy, *India: Progress or Poverty?*, Research Monograph 27, Institute of Economic Affairs, London, 1971.

Some of the most relevant contemporary studies are: B. Balassa, 'Reforming the system of incentives in developing countries', *World Development*, 3 (1975), pp. 365-82; 'Export incentives and export performance in developing countries: a comparative analysis', *Weltwirtschaftliches Archiv*, 114 (1978), pp. 24-61; *The process of industrial development and alternative development strategies*, Essays in International Finance No. 141, Princeton University, 1980; J. N. Bhagwati & P. Desai, *India: Planning for Industrialisation*, OECD, Paris: Oxford University Press, 1970; 'Socialism and Indian Economic Policy', *World Development*, 3 (1975), pp. 213-21; J. N. Bhagwati & T. N. Srinivasan, *Foreign-trade Regimes and Economic Development: India*, National Bureau of Economic Research, New York, 1975; Anne O. Krueger, 'Indian planning experience', in T. Morgan *et al.* (eds.), *Readings in Economic Development*, Wadsworth, California, 1963, pp. 403-20; 'The political economy of the rent-seeking society', *American Economic Review*, 64 (June 1974); *The Benefits and Costs of Import-substitution in India: a Microeconomic Study*, University of Minnesota Press, Minneapolis, 1975; *Growth, distortions and patterns of trade among many countries*, Studies in International Finance, Princeton University, 1977; Uma Lele, *Food-grain marketing in India: private performance and public policy*, Cornell University Press, Ithaca, 1971; T. W. Schultz (ed.), *Distortions in agricultural incentives*, Indiana University Press, Bloomington, 1978; V. Sukhatme, 'The utilization of high-yielding rice and wheat varieties in India: an economic assessment', University of Chicago PhD thesis, 1977.

[13]

if the basic and commonsensical lessons of political economy had been acknowledged early on in the history of the Indian Republic, we might have found today a much more prosperous economy and a much healthier body politic than is the case.

To argue this, it is first necessary to describe an economy where the pursuit of the individual good by rational agents is conducted within some set of orderly political institutions which is conducive to both civil peace and sustained mass prosperity. Accordingly, Part I of this short *Paper* begins by describing the broad and familiar features of what may be called a *neo-classical* or *liberal* model, and then proceeds briefly to contrast it with a model in which individual incentives and public institutions have been distorted from their efficient characterisations.

The practical question that arises is: Where in practice have independent India's policies led most conspicuously to distorted incentives and institutions? This will be the subject of Part III. Part II places the discussion in context by briefly describing a few relevant aspects of the political history of the Indian Republic.

I have argued elsewhere that every normative proposal for action is, in principle, open to question and criticism on the logical and factual grounds upon which it is founded. Whenever two people disagree about what ought to be done, it will be found either that at least one of them has made a mistake of logic or that they are also in disagreement about the facts of the case.[1] In Part IV, a tentative manifesto for political and economic reform in India is proposed, and I hope these proposals too will be subjected to critical scrutiny on the positive grounds upon which I shall seek to establish them.

---

[1] S. Roy, 'On liberty and economic growth: preface to a philosophy for India', University of Cambridge PhD thesis, 1982a, Chapters I and II; 'Knowledge and freedom in economic theory: Parts I and II', Centre for Study of Public Choice, V.P.I.&S.U., working papers, 1982b. My epistemological arguments have closely followed those of Renford Bambrough, *Moral Scepticism and Moral Knowledge*, Routledge and Kegan Paul, London, 1979.

Part I: Theory

2. EFFICIENT INCENTIVES AND INSTITUTIONS

A 'FACT' may be understood as the opposite of that which could have been the case but is not. A basic fact of the study of men and society – one which was acknowledged first by Aristotle and then, very importantly, by Adam Smith, and which has been emphasised in modern times by Friedrich Hayek – is that, while we are able to study and speak of the nature of human decision and action in general terms, we do not and cannot have a knowledge of how *particular* actions are moved by particular causes and circumstances.[1] We might certainly know, for instance, that every household in an economy views *some* horizons, wants to fulfil *some* aspirations, and faces *some* constraints. But if we were asked to specify what all these characteristics happened to be as a matter of fact at any one moment, we would certainly not be able to do so.

[1] Aristotle, *Ethica Nicomachea*, in Richard McKeon (ed.), *The Basic Works of Aristotle*, Random House, New York, 1941. We read: '. . . the whole account of matters of conduct must be given in outline and not precisely, as we said at the very beginning that the accounts we demand must be in accordance with the subject matter; matters concerned with conduct and questions of what is good for us have no fixity, any more than matters of health. The general account being of this nature, this account of particular cases is yet more lacking in exactness; for they do not fall under any art or precept but the agents themselves must in each case consider what is appropriate to the occasion, as happens also in the art of medicine or of navigation.' (1,104a2-a9.)
'. . . we do not deliberate even about all human affairs; for instance, no Spartan deliberates about the best constitution for the Scythians. For none of these things can be brought about by our own efforts. We deliberate about things that are in our power and can be done.' (1,112a28-30.)
Adam Smith, *An Inquiry into the Nature and Causes of the Wealth of Nations* (1776), eds. R. H. Campbell *et al.*, Liberty Classics, Indianapolis, 1981. We read: 'What is the species of domestick industry which his capital can employ, and of which the produce is likely to be of the greatest value, every individual, it is evident, can, in his local situation, judge much better than any statesman or lawgiver can do for him.' (Book IV. ii. 10, p. 456.)
In modern times, Friedrich Hayek has always kept this fact in the foreground of his thinking. In his *Individualism and Economic Order*, Routledge and Kegan Paul, London, 1949, we read, for example, of '. . . the constitutional limitation of man's knowledge and interests, the fact the he *cannot* know more than a tiny part of the whole of society and that therefore all that can enter into his motives are the immediate effects which his actions will have in the sphere he knows . . .' (p. 14.) The individual agent has a 'special knowledge of circumstances of the fleeting moment not known to others'; thus '. . . practically every individual has some advantage over all others because he possesses unique information of which beneficial use might be made, but of which use can be made only if the decisions depending on it are left to him or are made with his active co-operation.' (p. 80.)

Men are concerned almost wholly with (and are experts at) living their own lives as best they can – foraging for food, shelter and work, celebrating weddings and births, rearing children, and mourning deaths. For the most part, they are neither interested in, nor competent at judging, what others happen to be doing in their private lives. Neither benevolence nor envy extends much beyond a man's immediate vicinity, and, certainly, neither *can* extend to people he does not know or come to know of in the course of a lifetime.

This fact is also acknowledged in modern micro-economics, when it is said that, for the individual agent to be able to make decisions and act upon them, it is sufficient for him to know (besides his own desires, abilities and constraints) only of the relative prices prevailing locally of the goods and skills he wishes to trade.

'Efficient incentive' defined

We might then provisionally define an 'efficient incentive' as a set of relative prices and wages such that, when economic agents act upon them, three conditions are fulfilled:

(i) the difference between the total demand for and the total supply of every good and skill is zero;

(ii) every consumer succeeds in trading the amounts of different goods that he desires, and so obtains the highest utility he can within the constraint of his budget;

(iii) every private enterprise maximises the difference between its total revenues and total costs, that is, its profits.[1]

Rational action, however, occurs within a particular institutional context. Which action is rational and which is not will depend on what institutions there are and how well or poorly they function. As both classical liberals and Marxists argue, the neo-Walrasian tradition in modern economics – as exemplified by the Arrow-Debreu model – is practically devoid of any explicit institutional description, and so may best be regarded as a useful but grossly incomplete metaphor in the economist's inquiry.

[1] The mathematical economist will recognise these three conditions as the characteristics which define a multi-market general equilibrium in the Arrow-Debreu model: Gerard Debreu, *Theory of Value*, Yale University Press, New Haven, 1959; K. J. Arrow and F. H. Hahn, *General Competitive Analysis*, Oliver and Boyd, Edinburgh, 1971.

The institutions most relevant to economic activity are those of government. We might therefore add a fourth condition to characterise an efficient economy, namely, that government institutions work in such a way as to allocate tax revenues towards providing public goods in the amounts desired by citizens. This must be an institutional assumption implicit in the general equilibrium construction, without which it would be impossible to see the sense of that model.

The question that follows is how we are to ascertain the composition of the set of public goods to be provided. As is commonly known, this seems to confront the economist with numerous conceptual and practical problems. I propose here to circumvent all the typical difficulties of how to discover and combine individual preferences for public goods, or how to prevent free-riders, and to take a somewhat different route.

Functions of civil government : protection, public goods, education

To answer the question 'What should be public goods first and foremost?', I suggest we look for the kind of answer Adam Smith or Jeremy Bentham or J. S. Mill might have given to a related but different question: 'What should be the functions of government in a large civil society, regardless of whether or not it is constituted democratically?' This was the relevant question before the modern era of mass democracy. And it is still interesting because, first, it probably remains the appropriate question for the many countries today which either do not have democratic governments or do not have long histories of democracy, and, secondly, because the kinds of answer given by classical authors were very similar to those we might expect from individual citizens in modern democracies as well.

The most important practical functions of civil government include defence against external aggression, the dispensing of civil and criminal justice, the protection of life, property and trade – broadly, the Rule of Law – and the pursuit of a judicious foreign policy. All are different aspects of the same broad objective of ensuring the survival of the community and the security of individual life.

Yet no pretext has been more common than that an imminent danger to the security of the community requires the government to take despotic measures. The guarantee by a civil government

[17]

of the freedom of inquiry, discourse, criticism, and historical research should take precedence, therefore, even over ensuring security and survival, for it is probably the only final check there can be on whether what a government says is or is not in fact the case. Where this freedom is forcibly denied, or where it exists but people are too apathetic, ignorant or busy with their daily lives to exercise it, public life soon becomes self-deceptive and absurd, with propaganda taking the place of discourse, and pretensions and appearances diverging more and more from attainments and reality. Wherever the questions 'What is true?' or 'What is the case?' are not asked frequently enough, there will be fewer and fewer correct answers as to what the case happens to be.[1]

After collective and individual security, the functions of government include the building of dams, embankments, bridges and canals, the provision of roads and fresh water, and so on – activities which, as Adam Smith put it,

'. . . though they may be in the highest degree advantageous to a great society, are, however, of such a nature that the profit could never repay the expence to any individual or small number of individuals, and which it, therefore, cannot be expected that any individual or small number of individuals should erect or maintain'.[2]

Each may be more or less a 'pure' public good in the modern sense:

'that each individual's consumption of such a good leads to no subtraction from any other individual's consumption of that good'.[3]

Such a list could be extended to include activities as diverse as: the prevention of soil erosion; the public finance of school education, and of measures of basic public health such as vaccinations against contagious diseases; the issuing of currency; sewage disposal; population censuses; the standardisation of weights and measures; and so on. It is unnecessary to be more specific here since some people will find even this list controversial. Dogmatists will deny the need for free inquiry; pacifists will dispute that defence is a public good; communists will protest against the public protection of private property; 'anarcho-capitalists' will contest the

[1] This argument is discussed further in Roy (1982a), pp. 96-107, pp. 133-43.

[2] Adam Smith, *op. cit.*, Book V.i.c., p. 723.

[3] P. A. Samuelson, 'A pure theory of public expenditures', *Review of Economics & Statistics*, 36, 1954, reprinted in K. J. Arrow & T. Scitovsky (eds.), *Readings in Welfare Economics*, R. D. Irwin, Homewood, Ill., 1969.

public dispensation of justice; and so on. To these critics, I would offer merely the following short and incomplete reply.

First, a sound argument can be made that what functions civil government should have *can be* ascertained, without prejudice, by reasonable citizens, though which particular functions these are may well vary according to circumstances. Secondly, if we could spend time in thoughtful and leisured conversation with every citizen of a large community, it might be predicted – as a matter of cold, empirical fact – that practically everyone would agree with the suggestion that the first destinations of tax revenues should indeed be activities like defence, civil protection and the Rule of Law, the provision of roads, and so on. If such a prediction is correct, my thesis is plainly much more democratic than it might appear to modern economists, though I shall later claim that an objective defence of democratic institutions can be made on quite different grounds as well.

If there is a clear family resemblance between classical liberal authors – from Smith and Mill through to Hayek, Robbins, Friedman, Buchanan, Bauer and many others – it has to do, not so much with the denunciation of government activity in the market-place, as with the recognition of the existence of certain duties of government *outside* it, the fulfilment of which are indispensable to civil life, let alone the pursuit of economic prosperity. Their protest is at the high opportunity cost of the alternatives foregone.

This raises the question of how we might tell whether government is working well or badly in a particular country at a particular time, or, generally, how we might tell whether different public goods are provided in too small or large amounts. For present purposes it will again be sufficient to suggest a very rough and commonsense way of proceeding: let us *look* first, and think second. For example, the Iran-Iraq war has clearly been a perfect public bad as far as the ordinary citizenry in either country are concerned. Similarly, if there happen to be millions of cases queueing outside the courts waiting to be heard, or if crime is rampant and police protection ineffective, that may constitute *prima facie* evidence that too few public resources have been devoted to civil order and justice. Or, if heavy rainfall annually causes landslides in the hills and floods in the plains, devastating crops and leaving innumerable citizens destitute, that also might prompt us to ask whether sufficient public resources have gone towards precautions against such havoc. And so on.[1]

Which goods happen to be public goods depends on the circumstances and the level of government being discussed. For similar circumstances and levels, similar goods will most likely be public goods in different countries. The state ordinarily consists not only of the national government but also of several provincial governments and a myriad of local governments. In particular, a premise of the liberal state would be that public goods should *in fact* be provided by various levels of government, financed through taxes paid respectively at those levels. The citizen is a taxpayer at a variety of levels, and accordingly public goods are due to be provided at a variety of levels. Just as the national government may not usurp the power to tax for, or spend money on, a public good which is best provided by a provincial government to the citizens of a province, so a provincial government may not tax for, or spend on, a public good best provided by a local government to the citizens of a locality. The broad principle involved has two aspects: first, a recognition that knowledge of particular circumstances – and hence the ability *to act* – is infinitesimally dispersed within a population; and, secondly, as direct and visible a matching as possible of the benefits a citizen

---

[1] The idea I have in the background is of some implicit public goods function, endorsed more or less unanimously by *citizens* – but *not* necessarily by those with political power – with common sense dictating the elements it should contain. Thus:

Let $U=U\,(\pi_1, \pi_2, \ldots, \pi_k)$ be such a function, with $U'_i > 0$ and $U''_i < 0$, $i = 1,2,\ldots,k$, where π_i, $i = 1,2,\ldots k$, is a public good like defence, civil protection, roads, dams, or the finance of basic education which is produced, as it were, by the expenditure of tax revenues:

$$\pi_i = \pi_i(\tau_i),\ \pi'_i > 0,\ \pi''_i < 0,$$
$$\sum_{i=1}^{k} \tau_i = \bar{\tau}$$

where $\bar{\tau}$ is the total tax revenue available. The efficient conditions, i.e. in which the tax revenue is efficiently allocated among alternative public goods, would then be

$$\frac{\partial U/\partial \pi_i}{\partial \pi_i/\partial \tau_i} = \frac{\partial U/\partial \pi_j}{\partial \pi_j/\partial \tau_i} \qquad \text{for all } i,j = 1,2,\ldots,k.$$

So, if the marginal tax-rupee was put towards the production of any public good, the increase in social utility should be the same; otherwise we would find an excess supply of some public goods (e.g. bureaucrats) and an excess demand for others (e.g. courts, dams, police protection, etc.).

receives from a particular public good with the taxes he pays towards it, thereby perhaps reducing his incentive to be a free-rider on the contributions of others.

Uncertainty and ignorance

Provisionally, therefore, efficient incentives may be thought to consist of a set of market-clearing relative prices and wages, occurring within an institutional context in which the basic and indispensable functions of government have been adequately performed at a variety of appropriate levels.

Such a definition would still be seriously incomplete in one major respect. For we must now recognise: (i) that history is unique and irretrievable, that the present consists only of the fleeting moment, and that the future, by its very nature, cannot be fully known; (ii) that such a thing as human freedom exists; and (iii) that, as a consequence, uncertainty and ignorance are ubiquitous.

Some of the uncertainty derives from the unfolding of natural events (like the rains) over which man has little or no control. The rest derives from the fact that the individual is a free agent who is affected by the actions of others but who cannot predict those actions completely because they too are free agents like himself. Game theory would have had no appeal for the economist if the existence of human freedom had not been a fact. It is this which makes it impossible to read everything in another person's mind and thus makes it impossible to predict everything he might do. The lasting contribution of Keynesian economics could be its emphasis that such uncertainty and ignorance are important to the economist's inquiry.

Mathematical economists have been saying for several years that what is required if we are to be realistic are models which reflect the sequential character of actual decision-making and account for the past being immutable and the future uncertain.[1] However, they have proceeded to write even more complex mathematics than we already have – disregarding Aristotle's advice not to seek more precision from the subject of an inquiry than it

[1] Two examples are F. H. Hahn, *On the notion of equilibrium in economics: an inaugural lecture*, Cambridge University Press, Cambridge, 1973, and J. M. Grandmont, 'Temporary general equilibrium theory: a survey', *Econometrica*, vol. 46, 1977.

may be capable of yielding.[1] My question is the more mundane one of what becomes of the classical liberals' concept of efficient incentives and institutions in a dynamic world. I shall answer it too in a pedestrian way.

The single overwhelming reason why uncertainty and ignorance are relevant to the economist's descriptions is that they make real the possibility of *mistakes* by economic agents. To extend the previous discussion to a dynamic context, what we can do is to ask which institutions are most likely to reduce or mitigate the social consequences of mistaken decisions, whether made by private agents or by those in public office. And it is here that the classical liberals advocate two important institutional features: competition and the decentralisation of decision-making.

The major value of democratic institutions over authoritarian ones is that they encourage these two principles to be put into effect. Because, in a large economy, particular knowledge is infinitesimally dispersed, it may be better for adjustments to a multitude of variables to be made continuously in response to changing circumstances by a vast number of small economic agents, rather than for adjustments to a few variables to be made at political intervals by a small group of very powerful agents. The concentration of power to make major decisions among a few fallible men is a much more ominous prospect than the distribution of power in small amounts among a large number of fallible men. It is much more dangerous for a monopoly of ideas to be claimed about where the political good of a country lies than for there to be free and open competition among such ideas at the bar of reason.

D. H. Robertson put it well when he warned

'. . . that all the eggs should not be in the same basket – that in this highly uncertain world the fortunes of a whole trade, or a whole area, should not depend on the foresight and judgement of a single centre of decision'.[2]

The presumption in favour of democratic institutions is that they reduce the potential damage from wrong political decisions –

[1] Aristotle, *op. cit.*, 1,094b12-1,094b27.

[2] D. H. Robertson, 'The Economic Outlook', in his *Utility and All That*, Allen & Unwin, London, 1952, pp. 51-52.

damage which can be rationally expected in an uncertain world.[1] Elections, in the liberal understanding, are then not so much the means to promote the interests of one's confederates as to remove from office without bloodshed rulers who fail to do what they are entrusted with, and to replace them by those from whom better is expected.

Economic efficiency in an uncertain world

The economic notion of efficient incentives is also modified by uncertainty and ignorance. In the theory, a set of prices is market-clearing only relative to unchanging preferences, resources and technologies. In a dynamic world, however, demand and supply functions are themselves changing and the notion of efficient incentives must accordingly be adapted to one in which relative prices *move* in the direction of the excess demand: that is, if the parameters change so that the total demand for a good or skill comes to exceed the total supply, we should want to see its relative price rising (and, conversely, if total supply exceeds total demand, we should want to see its relative price falling). During such a process of adjustment, many people may suffer very considerable hardship – something which reasonable Keynesians do well to emphasise.

If changing preferences, resources or technologies cause the demand for a product to diminish, we should want to see the firms which manufacture it either entering different markets, or improving its quality by technological innovation, or lowering prices. Similarly, we should want to see workers in these firms – whether blue- or white-collar – who have skills specific to a product whose price is falling either increasing their productivity or retraining themselves in different skills more specific to the manufacture of goods whose prices are rising. Numerous enter-

[1] Karl Popper made a similar point in *The Open Society and its Enemies*, Princeton University Press, Princeton, 1950, when he suggested that Plato's question 'Who should rule?' should be discarded for the question: 'How can we so organise political institutions that bad or incompetent rulers can be prevented from doing too much damage?' (p. 120). There is relevant discussion by Renford Bambrough in 'Plato's modern friends and enemies', *Philosophy*, 37, 1962, reprinted in R. Bambrough (ed.), *Plato, Popper and Politics: some contributions to a modern controversy*, Barnes and Noble, New York, 1967. I have discussed the relationship of expertise to democracy in Roy (1982a), pp. 80-95.

prises can go bankrupt, and numerous workers can find themselves unable to sell the skills they possess, if they fail to adapt quickly enough to changing market conditions. The more specialised the product and the more specific the skill, the more hardship there may be. There could well be orthodox Keynesian consequences whereby laid-off workers reduce their consumption expenditures and firms on the verge of bankruptcy reduce their investment expenditures, leading to lower incomes for others, and thus to lower expenditures by them too, and so on. An anti-Keynesian who denied the existence of such hardship would be closed to the facts. He might also not be doing his own theory justice: for it is not unreasonable to argue that, while adjustments are inevitable in an uncertain world, the classical response of prices moving in the direction of excess demand probably minimises the hardship in the transition from one equilibrium to the next.

In a dynamic world, therefore, in which supply and demand functions are shifting continually and unpredictably (though probably incrementally, and not drastically), efficient incentives are better thought of as relative prices which are not stagnant but which are moving – and moving quickly – in the direction of excess demand. It should, in general, be continually profitable at the margin for firms and workers to be innovating technologically and improving productivity. As everyone knows from experience, the principle goad to such activity is fair and free competition. If a job or contract is sought badly enough, and if better quality or lower price are known to be the only criteria of selection, the expected outcome is a differentiation and improvement by competitors of the individual quality or price of what is sold.

In broad summary, the liberal understanding of how material well-being can be improved rests on the assumption that the basic functions of civil government are performed satisfactorily. Government provides the backdrop of civil order and protection necessary for private citizens freely and fairly to conduct their own lives and their transactions with one another. It is a theory which acknowledges a fundamental fact in the study of society, namely, that the individual household: (a) most commonly defines its own horizons; (b) knows the particular opportunities available to it to produce, trade and consume; (c) recognises the particular constraints which prevent it from doing all that it may desire; and

[24]

(d) perceives how these opportunities and constraints may be changing. Where, as in the liberal picture, there are large numbers of producers and consumers, sellers and buyers – each family acting more or less independently – the efforts of one family do not directly make for other than its own success, while at the same time the repercussions of its mistakes are felt by itself and do not reverberate throughout the whole community. Such has been, as I see it, the American secret to mass prosperity.

3. DISTORTED INCENTIVES AND INSTITUTIONS

DISTORTED INCENTIVES are the logical opposites of efficient ones. Relative prices and wages send distorted signals to individual economic agents when they do not move in the direction of excess demand, so that there is no general tendency for markets to clear. A long-run or endemic excess demand for a good reveals itself in rationing, queueing and black markets. The price at which trade nominally takes place is too low and shows no tendency to move upwards.

Conversely, in a product market, a long-run or endemic excess supply reveals itself in surpluses and spoilages. In a labour market, it reveals itself, on the one hand, in armies of tenured employees who have no incentive to improve productivity, and, on the other hand, in lines of involuntarily or disguised unemployed who cannot sell all the skills they possess and have to settle for selling their less-specialised ones. The price at which trade nominally takes place is too high and shows no tendency to move downwards. In practical terms, firms do not find it profitable to be continually entering new markets or improving quality or enhancing technology or reducing price in order to attract and retain customers. Farmers in particular may face output and input prices which make technological improvements unprofitable.

In politics, distorted incentives are ones which make it profitable for politicians and government officials to be corruptible and taxpayers to be evasive. Because corruption is not penalised and honesty not rewarded, the pursuit of private interest may make it rational to be corrupt and irrational to be honest.

[25]

Individualism and statism

A neo-classical economic model like the one outlined above presupposes among citizens a political attitude of *individualism*. This may be defined as a condition in which citizens have the idea (a) that it is the individual household itself which is principally responsible for improvements in its own well-being, and (b) that government merely

> 'is, or ought to be, instituted for the common benefit, protection and security of the people . . .',[1]

and that government officials are merely the citizens' 'trustees and servants, and at all times amenable to them'.[1]

Its logical opposite may be called an attitude of *statism* – defined as prevailing when various classes of citizens have the idea that it is government which is and should be principally responsible for improvements in individual and public well-being. A good sense in which 'power' can be defined in political and economic contexts is as 'the capacity to restrict the choices open to other men'.[2] An attitude of statism entails a willingness, or at least an acquiescence, on the part of citizens to relinquish to those in government, with little or no questioning, the power to make decisions which may affect their lives intimately. At the same time, responsibility for relapses or lack of progress in individual well-being is also thought to be the consequence of governmental and not private decision-making. Whereas individualism is a self-assertive attitude, statism is a self-abnegating one. For those in government to have a statist mentality is the same as saying they are paternalistic, that is, making the presumption that the citizen is often incapable of judging for himself what is for his own good.

The suggestion that government should have the principal responsibility for improvements in individual and collective economic well-being – in the sense that the collectivity can and should satisfy the material aspirations of every individual – appears straightaway to be self-contradictory. An individual can have

[1] Virginia Bill of Rights, 1776, in *The Constitution of the United States*, ed. E. C. Smith, Barnes & Noble, New York, 1979, p. 21.

[2] P. T. Bauer, *Dissent on Development*, Harvard University Press, Cambridge, Mass., 1971, p. 72, n. 2. The term 'statism' suggested itself to the author after he read M. R. Masani, 'Post-Sanjay outlook: where salvation does not lie', *The Statesman*, 9 July 1980.

enough difficulty trying to articulate his own horizons, aspirations and constraints, let alone trying to do the same for others. For a politician (or economist) to claim (or imply) not only that he knows (or can know) the relevant characteristics of everyone at once, but also that he knows how to ameliorate the condition of humanity at a stroke, as if by magic, would have been considered ridiculous in more candid times than ours. If we understand 'collective effort' to mean the sum of individual labours engaged in a common pursuit or endeavour, then for the collectivity to try materially to satisfy every individual would amount to imposing a duty on everyone to try materially to satisfy everyone *else* – an absurd state of affairs, flying in the face of the fact that most people most of the time do not wish to, or cannot, cope with much else except their private lives.

Exhorting government directly to improve the material well-being of 'the people' cannot mean what it seems to because it cannot refer to literally *all* the people but only to *some* of them – perhaps only a majority, or only the well-organised. That the state is endogenous to the polity implies that no government has resources of its own out of which to disburse the amounts a politician may promise or an economist recommend. To fulfil new promises, given an initial condition of budgetary equilibrium, a government is only able *either* to print more fiat money *or* to tax the resources of individual citizens more heavily. Leaving aside the first alternative, fulfilment of the exhortation amounts to using public institutions to transfer resources from some people in order to keep promises made to others.

When the attitude spreads that, in politics, one man's gain is another man's loss, and where political control is to be had by winning majorities in elections, the citizen comes to face a perverse incentive to try to coalesce with more and more others in the hope of capturing the public revenues in his favour – instead of thinking critically about the nature of the political good as the institutions of democracy require him to. Political power becomes less dispersed, and the size of the polity diminishes in the sense that it comes to have fewer and fewer constituent agents, each of which is a larger and larger coalition of like-minded confederates intent on acquiring control for its own benefit.

Perhaps the worst consequence of a general attitude of statism, however, is that the basic, commonsensical functions of government are obscured, ignored, and neglected. Instead of requiring politicians and government officials to fulfil these functions, a citizenry allows its public agents to become brokers and entrepreneurs – trading not only in the products of government-controlled industries but also in an array of positions of power and privilege, all in the name of directing a common endeavour to help the poor. The state places itself at every profitable opportunity between private citizens who might otherwise have conducted their transactions themselves perfectly well. The result is that governments do, or try to do, what either does not need to be done or ought not to be done by government, while they neglect that which only governments can do and which therefore they ought to be doing.

Part II: History

4. INDIVIDUALISM AND STATISM IN INDIA

AN ATTITUDE of statism has probably been present in India since Mughal times at least. If anything, it spread during the British period since the *raison d'être* of British rule in India would have vanished without paternalism (as in the course of time it did) and the existence of British rule was the *raison d'être* of the nationalist movement.

Paternalism towards India was espoused even by those Englishmen known for their liberal views at home. Thomas Macaulay, for instance, declared to the House of Commons in 1833:

'It may be that the public mind of India may expand under our system till it has outgrown that system; that by good government we may educate our subjects into a capacity for better government; that having become instructed in European knowledge, they may, in some future stage, demand European institutions. Whether such a day will ever come I know not. But never will I attempt to avert or retard it. Whenever it comes, it will be the proudest day in English history.'[1]

[1] G. M. Young (ed.), *Macaulay: Prose and Poetry*, London: Macmillan, 1952, p. 718. Some 20 years later, in *Considerations on Representative Government*,

[*Continued on p. 29*]

[28]

Less than a hundred years later, in 1930-31, the Indian National Congress – to the considerable chagrin of the British Government – resolved to bring about an independent India in which every citizen would have the right to free speech, to profess and practise his faith freely, and to move and practise his profession anywhere in the country. There would be universal adult suffrage and no-one would be unjustly deprived of his liberty or have his property entered, sequestered or confiscated. In particular, all citizens in the future republic would be 'equal before the law, irrespective of religion, caste, creed or sex', and no disability would attach

> 'to any citizen by reason of his or her religion, caste, creed or sex, in regard to public employment, office of power or honour, and in the exercise of any trade or calling'.[1]

These resolutions were made in the thick of the battle for independence, and underscored the fundamental argument of the nationalists that, in spite of the infinitely diverse characteristics of the inhabitants of the sub-continent, a free and secular India was possible in which all would be ruled by a common law. That argument had been in contradistinction to the frequent taunt from British Conservatives that an India without Britain would disintegrate in internecine bloodshed, and also to the later 'two-nations' theory of the Muslim League which led eventually to the creation of Pakistan. With the departure of the British and the Pakistanis, in 1950 the Constitution of the first Indian Republic was finally able to bring into force the idea of secularity which had inspired the nationalist cause. Thus, among the Fundamental Rights established by the Constitution, Article 14 provided that the state

> 'shall not deny to any person equality before the law or the equal protection of the laws within the territory of India'.

[Continued from p. 28]
    ed. H. B. Acton (London: J. M. Dent), J. S. Mill claimed that rule by 'a superior people . . . is often of the greatest advantage to a people, carrying them rapidly through several stages of progress' (Ch. IV, p. 224). Ironically, a few years ago a distinguished retired member of the Indian civil service (who happens to be a recipient of the Lenin Peace Prize) used very similar words in a newspaper article – in defence of the Soviet occupation of Afghanistan!

[1] Resolution of the Indian National Congress, August 1931, reprinted in B. N. Pandey (ed.), *The Indian Nationalist Movement: 1885-1947*, Macmillan, London, 1979, p. 67.

Articles 15.1, 15.2, 16.1, 16.2 and 29.2 went on to prohibit discrimination on the arbitrary grounds of religion, race, caste, sex or place of birth in matters of public employment or access to publicly-funded education.

The century between Macaulay and the resolutions for independence was by far the most important to the country's intellectual history since earliest antiquity. While it took its turbulent course, India's connections with the mind of Europe – long severed since the time of the early Greeks – came to be re-established. The common interest and the common contribution became one of admiring and learning from Europe and from India's own past what there was to be admired and learnt, whilst forsaking and resisting what was self-contradictory or base. The maxim for a century might have been: learn the good and let the evil be buried in history. As Tagore wrote:

> 'The lamp of Europe is still burning; we must rekindle our old and extinguished lamp at that flame and start again on the road of time. We must fulfil the purpose of our connection with the English. This is the task we face in the building up of a great India.'[1]

The ideal aspired to was *swaraj*, or 'self-rule'. It literally meant not only a government of India by Indians accountable to Indians, but also the governance of the individual *by himself*. Not only was the country to be sovereign *vis-à-vis* other states; its individual citizens were to be free *vis-à-vis* each other and equal before its laws. *Swaraj* meant, in other words, a condition of political autonomy where the citizen constrained his own free actions so as not to harm others, and where the Rule of Law would protect him when he acted autonomously and resist him when he did not. Given a backdrop of civil order, the infinite number of ways to individual happiness and prosperity in an infinitely diverse sub-continent could then be pursued.

[1] S. Radhakrishnan, *The philosophy of Rabindranath Tagore*, Macmillan, London, 1918, p. 232. For an excellent account of the intercourse between ancient India and ancient Greece, H. G. Rawlinson, 'Early contacts between India and Europe', in A. L. Basham (ed.), *A Cultural History of India*, Clarendon Press, Oxford, 1975. For excellent accounts of the growth of liberalism in India in the 19th and early 20th centuries: Anil Seal, *The Emergence of Indian Nationalism: Competition and Collaboration in the later 19th Century*, Cambridge University Press, Cambridge, 1971, Chs. 1, 3-6; J. R. McLane, *Indian Nationalism and the Early Congress*, Princeton University Press, Princeton, 1977; Gordon Johnson, *Provincial Politics and Indian Nationalism*, Cambridge University Press, Cambridge, 1973, Ch. 1.

Statism all-pervading

An attitude of statism, however, has pervaded all public discourse in independent India, and has been reinforced by the social and economic policies pursued by successive governments.

In the first place, a ghost from earlier controversies with the British was to remain in the 1950 Constitution. Immediately after the provisions establishing equality before the law and equality of opportunity in public employment and publicly-funded education, the following caveats appeared. Article 15.3 said that the state could make 'any special provision for women and children'; and then, of more significance, Article 15.4 allowed the state to make

'any special provisions for the advancement of any socially and educationally backward classes of citizens or for the Scheduled Castes and the Scheduled Tribes'.

Article 16.4 allowed it to make

'any provision for the reservation of appointments or posts in favour of any backward class of citizens which, in the opinion of the State, is not adequately represented in the services under the State . . .'.

Lastly, Article 335 said that

'the claims of the members of the Scheduled Castes and the Scheduled Tribes shall be taken into consideration, consistently with the maintenance of efficiency of administration, in the making of appointments to services and posts [under the State] . . .'.

Who was to decide who was 'backward' and who was not, or which group was to be 'scheduled' and which not? Article 341.1 said that

'The President may . . . by public notification specify the castes, races or tribes which shall for the purposes of this Constitution be deemed to be Scheduled Castes . . .';

and Article 341.2 added that

'Parliament may by law include in or exclude from the list of Scheduled Castes specified under 341.1 any caste, race or tribe or part of or any group within any caste, race or tribe . . .'.

Articles 342.1 and 342.2 said the same for the Scheduled Tribes.

[31]

Subsequently, two Presidential Orders named no fewer than 1,181 different groups in the country as 'Scheduled Castes' and more than 583 other groups as 'Scheduled Tribes'. Roughly a sixth of the population thus came to be termed 'backward' by executive decree and were segregated by statute from the rest of the citizenry.

The direct precursor of these provisions was the 'Communal Award' by the British Government in 1932, who had taken it to be their duty

'to safeguard what we believe to be the right of Depressed Classes to a fair proportion in Legislatures . . .'.[1]

('Depressed Classes' was the official name for those misleadingly called 'untouchables' outside the Hindu fold.)

The complex customs of the Hindus call for endogamy and commensality among members of the same caste, thus making anyone outside a caste somewhat 'untouchable' for its members. In marriage and dining habits, many orthodox Hindus would hold foreigners, Muslims, and even Hindus of other castes at the same distance as those formally classified as 'Depressed Classes'. Indeed, non-Hindus in India – including the British – often maintained social protocols that were equally as strict.

No serious Indian historian would doubt that members of the 'Depressed Classes' had been oppressed and had suffered countless indignities throughout Indian history at the hands of so-called 'caste Hindus'. At various times, persecution had led to mass conversions to the more secular faiths. But the ancient wrongs of the Hindu practices had to do not so much with the lack of physical contact in personal life which the word 'untouchability' connotes – for Indian society has always consisted of a myriad of voluntarily-segregated groups – but rather with open and obvious inequities such as the denial of equal access to temples, public wells, baths and schools.

Gandhi, who by his personal example probably did more for the cause of the 'Depressed Classes' than anyone else, protested against the Communal Award with one of his most famous fasts. Privately, he suspected that

---

[1] Ramsay Macdonald's letter to M. K. Gandhi, 8 September 1932, reprinted in Pandey (ed.), *op. cit.*, p. 74.

[32]

'. . . the communal question [was] being brought deliberately to the forefront and magnified by the government because they did not intend to part with power'.[1]

Publicly, he argued that the pernicious consequence would be a further exacerbation of the *apartheid* under which the 'Depressed Classes' had suffered for so long, when the important thing was for their right to be within the Hindu fold to be acknowledged by 'caste' Hindus.[2]

The Fundamental Rights in the 1950 Constitution establishing the *equality* of all citizens before the law evidently had the 1930-31 resolutions as their precursors; while Article 17 – which specifically declared 'untouchability' to be 'abolished' and its practice 'forbidden' – was part of Gandhi's legacy, placing those who had for centuries been denigrated and persecuted on exactly the same footing in the eyes of the laws of the Republic as their denigrators and persecutors. The subsequent clauses authorising the state to discriminate in favour of 'Scheduled Castes', and allowing it to define by executive decree who was to be so called, were evidently the remnants of the Communal Award of 1932. Discrimination by the state was initially to last for a period of 10 years only. It has, however, been extended three times – for another 10 years on each occasion – and so continues to the present day. We shall examine a few of the consequences in Part III.

'A socialistic pattern of society'

As for economic policy, while the original 1950 Constitution had ambiguously stated certain ends – such as that government was 'to strive to promote the welfare of the people' – it made no mention at all of any specific economic institutions, statist or liberal, which the new Republic was to nurture as means towards

[1] Devdas Gandhi's letter to Jawaharlal Nehru, 2 October 1931, reprinted in Pandey (ed.), *op. cit.*, p. 71.

[2] Gandhi's protest succeeded to the extent that the Award itself was superseded; and in unusual, euphoric displays of fraternity, 'caste' Hindus threw open temples to members of the 'Depressed Classes' and embraced them with garlands. The compromise Pact which replaced the Communal Award removed separate electorates but still guaranteed special political representation for some years following the agreement. For an account of Gandhi's position on the Communal Award, Judith M. Brown, *Gandhi and Civil Disobedience*, Cambridge University Press, Cambridge, 1977, pp. 313-21.

those ends. In spite of this omission, successive governments have explicitly avowed their espousal of 'socialism' as the means to the good and prosperous society. For instance, a

'socialistic pattern of society where the principal means of production are under social ownership or control'

was declared to be a national objective at the ruling Congress Party's convention in 1955; and, in 1976, the notorious 42nd Amendment purported to change the very description of the country in the preamble to the original Constitution from the sober 'Sovereign, Democratic Republic' to the awkward 'Sovereign, Secular, Socialist Democratic Republic'. It is an open and important issue of constitutional practice whether a temporary majoritarian government can change the legal description of a republic so fundamentally that it necessarily begs every question now and in the future about the efficacy of socialism as the route to mass prosperity.[1]

Even so, 'socialism' is a vague and equivocal word, meaning different things to different people. Briefly, what happened in the Indian context seems to have been that the Nationalist Government explicitly took upon itself the responsibility of becoming the prime mover of the economic growth of the country. This was in addition to its other fundamental and urgent political responsibilities at the time, namely, to establish peace and civil order in the aftermath of a bloody partition, re-settle several million destitute refugees, integrate into the Republic the numerous principalities and fiefdoms run by the princes and potentates, re-draw provincial boundaries on a sensible linguistic criterion, and generally educate people about their rights and responsibilities as individual citizens in a new and democratic republic.

In a poor country which had just ended a long period of alien rule, it was understandable, if inadvisable, that a nationalist government led by cultured, educated men among unlettered masses should take upon itself the responsibility for economic growth. Part of the nationalists' critique of British rule had been precisely that it had worked to the considerable detriment of the Indian economy. And, certainly, whatever the exact calculation

[1] For an eminent lawyer's commentary, N. A. Palkhivala, *The Light of the Constitution*, Forum of Free Enterprise, Bombay, 1976.

of the benefits and costs of the British presence in India, while there had been obvious benefits, there had also been obvious costs such as iniquitous taxes and overt racial discrimination in employment.[1] Thus, when the nationalists practically swore themselves to provide better government for the economy, it was certainly a very praiseworthy aim; 1947 would indeed be the year of India's 'tryst with destiny'.

Better government not necessarily more government

What the Nehru Government came to believe, however, was that better government for the economy necessarily meant *more* government activity in the economy. A similar nationalist government led by cultured, educated men among an unlettered public had chosen differently in 1776 at Philadelphia, but the times and circumstances were very different. The Indian nationalists, and most especially Prime Minister Nehru, had just witnessed what they took to be, on the one hand, the collapse of the market economy in the Great Depression and, on the other, the rapid growth to greatness of Bolshevik Russia. In his presidential address to the Congress in 1936, for instance, Nehru spoke of the immediate past in these terms:

'Everywhere conflicts grew, and a great depression overwhelmed the world and there was a progressive deterioration, everywhere except in the wideflung Soviet territories of the USSR, where, in marked contrast with the rest of the world, astonishing progress was made in every direction . . .'

Thus, it seemed to him, there was

'. . . no way of ending the poverty, the vast unemployment, the degradation, and the subjection of the Indian people except through Socialism'.

Socialism meant, *inter alia*,

'. . . the ending of private property, except in a restricted sense, and the replacement of the private profit system by a higher ideal of

---

[1] There is reason to think the Mughals before the British had done no better and had probably done much worse. (T. Raychaudhuri, 'The State and the Economy: the Mughal Empire', in T. Raychaudhuri & I. Habib (eds.), *The Cambridge Economic History of India*, vol. I, Cambridge University Press, Cambridge, 1982.

co-operative service. It means ultimately a change in our instincts and habits and desires. In short, it means a new civilisation, radically different from the present capitalist order. Some glimpse we can have of this new civilisation in the territories of the USSR. Much has happened there which has pained me greatly and with which I disagree, but I look upon that great and fascinating unfolding of a new order and a new civilisation as the most promising feature of our dismal age. If the future is full of hope it is largely because of Soviet Russia and what it has done, and I am convinced that, if some world catastrophe does not intervene, this new civilisation will spread to other lands and put an end to the wars and conflicts on which capitalism feeds'.[1]

Equally as certain and deep as his admiration for the liberal values of the West was Nehru's evident misunderstanding of the causes and consequences of Stalin's Russia. The political and economic history of India in the past 30 years cannot be understood without regard to her most powerful leader's ambivalence about the nature of the political and economic good.

By the mid-1950s, many of India's other prominent statesmen had died or retired from public life, and there was hardly a public figure of stature left (with the exception of Rajagopalachari) to challenge Nehru's socialist vision of the country's future. Moreover, men who were ostensibly 'expert economists', but whose writings revealed no knowledge of prices or markets or the concept of feasibility, were encouraged to endorse and embellish this vision, which they did without hesitation in the secure knowledge that they were shielded from critics by the intellectual patronage of a charismatic and elected leader.[2]

The choice between alternative models of mass economic prosperity must have seemed quite clear at the time. The cold

[1] V. B. Singh (ed.), *Nehru on Socialism*, Government of India, Ministry of Information and Broadcasting, Publications Division, Delhi, 1977, pp. 56-57, 67.
[2] 'Draft recommendations for the formulation of the Second Five Year Plan', written by P. C. Mahalanobis; 'The Second Five-Year Plan – A tentative framework', drafted by the economic ministries; and a 'Memorandum' written by a panel of prominent Indian economists – all contained in *Papers relating to the formulation of the Second Five Year Plan*, Government of India: Planning Commission, 1955 – were the principal influences on the actual Second Plan. No significant understanding of markets, prices or the concept of feasibility is evident on the part of any of the authors. Shenoy's lonely dissent has already been noted (above, p. 13, note 1).

fact did not, however, vanish that one of the oldest objective lessons of political economy has been that more government is not necessarily better government. It is to the consequences of ignoring this lesson that we now turn.

Part III: Practice

5. ECONOMIC POLICIES IN INDEPENDENT INDIA

INDIA TODAY is a bizarre maze of distorted incentives, which I (and no doubt others) have found very difficult to untangle and understand. I shall, however, list and discuss the most significant of them as methodically as I can.

(i) *Industry*

The Indian Government has declared a large 'public sector' in commerce and industry to be a national objective. Towards this end, it has therefore progressively acquired numerous enterprises, large and small, so that it now has either a full monopoly in an industry or is one of a few oligopolists. These industries range from banking, insurance, railways, airlines, cement, steel, chemicals, fertilisers and ship-building to making beer, soft drinks, telephones and wrist-watches. There are no explicit penalties for indefinite loss-making; indeed, bankrupt private enterprises have often been nationalised to serve politicians' ends. And, certainly, there has been no general rule of marginal-cost pricing. In public utilities, like electricity generation and distribution or city buses and trams, prices appear to be well below marginal cost, leading to severe rationing and queueing. Sudden stoppages of electricity for hours at a time and monumental congestion on buses and trams have become endemic facts of life for millions of urban Indians.

At the same time, private industry in India has been made to

[37]

face labyrinthine controls. The government has continually exhorted private firms to work in the 'national interest' – which means accepting the constraints of centralised planning. It has left no doubt that, while there is a 'role' for them in the growth of the economy, they exist at the sufferance of government and had better realise it, otherwise the dark forces of revolution which have so far been kept at bay will inevitably sweep them away altogether, as happened in Russia and China.

The constraints imposed on the operation of a private business are legion, and would make a businessman from the West or Far East reach for a psychiatrist or a pistol. An entrepreneur may not enter numerous industries without government approval of the 'technical' viability of his project; once it is approved, he cannot find credit except from a government bank; and he cannot buy raw materials and machinery of the highest quality at the lowest price since, if they are produced in India, he will be denied a licence to import better and/or cheaper foreign substitutes. The onus is on him to satisfy the government that no production occurs within India of the input he requires; only then will an import licence conceivably be granted, subject to periodic review by the government. He may be compelled to export a specified proportion of his output as a condition for the renewal of his import licence, which therefore places him at a disadvantage with foreign buyers who, of course, are aware of this restraint. He may be unable to compete internationally because the rupee is priced above its likely equilibrium and some of the inputs he uses are high-cost, low-quality domestic substitutes. As a result, he may be compelled practically to dump his output abroad at whatever price it will fetch.

The entrepreneur's factory may be subject to random cuts in electricity for hours at a time. He may require government approval before he can increase his fixed capacity, modernise his plant, change a product-line, or even change the number of labour shifts. He may face minimum-wage and stringent unfair-dismissal laws on the one hand, and price controls on the other. If he fails to meet credit obligations to the nationalised banks, he may be penalised by the appointment of one or more government directors to his board – a form of 'creeping' nationalisation. Further, he may be subjected to a constant threat of full nationalisation as and when the government decides that his industry

[38]

should be in the public sector in the interests of national planning.[1]

The consequence of all these controls has been a monumental distortion of incentives away from encouraging private firms to try to attract customers by improving technology and quality or reducing prices towards encouraging them to concentrate on 'rent-seeking', in the term made familiar by Professors Gordon Tullock and James Buchanan.[2] As Anne Krueger says in her excellent study of the automobile ancillary industry, the very notion of entrepreneurial efficiency changes in such circumstances:

> 'Under conditions in India, the most important problem confronting entrepreneurs is that of assuring that production will continue. The combined effects of import licensing and investment licensing give virtually every firm a monopoly or quasi-monopoly position. The entrepreneur who is most successful in getting licences of greater value and/or in getting licences more quickly than his fellow producers will have higher profits. The producer who does not compete successfully for licences cannot produce at all, no matter how skilled he is in achieving engineering efficiency, unless he enters the "open market" and pays a premium to the successful licence applicant for some materials . . . Successful entrepreneurs are therefore those who are best at obtaining the greatest number of licences most expeditiously . . .'[3]

Moreover, firms which are low-cost and efficient (in the free-market sense) *and* which are as successful at rent-seeking as high-cost, inefficient firms may still not be able to compete the latter out of business because government will not usually allow a particular firm to expand – regardless of its efficiency – if there is excess capacity in the industry of which it is a part. High-cost firms can thereby rationally count on staying in business simply by maintaining significant excess capacity.

---

[1] The best descriptions of Indian industrial policy are still to be found in Bhagwati and Desai (1970), *op. cit.* Also C. Wadhwa, 'New Industrial Licensing Policy: An Appraisal', in C. Wadhwa (ed.), *Some problems of India's economic policy*, Tata-McGraw Hill, Delhi, 1977, pp. 290-324.

[2] Gordon Tullock is generally credited with introducing the notion of rent-seeking in 'The welfare costs of tariffs, monopolies and theft', *Western Economic Journal*, 5 (June 1967), while Krueger (1974), *op. cit.*, introduced the term itself. The collection edited by J. M. Buchanan *et al.*, *Toward a theory of the rent-seeking society*, Texas A&M Press, College Station, 1980, contains reprints of both papers as well as other studies.

[3] Krueger (1975), *op. cit.*, p. 108 ff.

(ii) *Foreign trade*

The Government of India has always claimed that foreign exchange is a 'scarce' resource which must be rationed by fiat in the national interest. The total foreign-exchange revenue (at an exchange rate which was fixed until 1971 and has since been on a managed 'peg') has been allocated in the following order of priorities: first, to meet foreign debt repayments and government expenditures in the conduct of foreign policy, such as the maintenance of embassies (G1); secondly, to pay for imports of defence equipment, food, fertilisers and petroleum (G2); thirdly, to meet ear-marked payments for the imported inputs of public-sector industries so that they may achieve projected production targets (G3); fourthly, to pay for the imported inputs of private-sector firms which are successful in obtaining import licences (P1); and, lastly, to satisfy the demands of the public at large for purposes such as travel abroad (P2).

Foreign exchange is 'scarce' in India, or elsewhere, in precisely the same sense that rice or petrol or cloth is scarce. Just as there exists some positive price for rice, petrol or cloth which, at any moment, will match total supplies with total demands, so there exists some positive price for rupees relative to dollars which, at any moment, will match the transaction and asset demands of Indians for dollars with the transaction and asset demands of foreigners for rupees. Underlying that market-clearing price would be (a) the demands of Indians for foreign goods whose f.o.b. prices were lower than those of domestic substitutes, and, similarly, the demands of foreigners for goods in which India has had a comparative advantage; and (b) the expectations of Indians and foreigners about the future purchasing power of the rupee relative to the dollar, using as a proxy, say, the difference between interest rates in India and abroad.

A free market in foreign exchange would first have encouraged India's traditional exports, like jute manufactures and textiles, and then (if the positive theory of international trade is broadly correct) progressively encouraged the export of other non-traditional goods which used India's relatively inexpensive labour relatively intensively and thereby enabled Indian entrepreneurs to compete successfully in foreign markets. At the same time, capital flows into and out of India would have given the monetary authorities an incentive to keep domestic interest rates in line with the

[40]

real opportunity cost of forgoing consumption in favour of savings.

Thus, the case against a free market in foreign exchange has always been, to say the least, far from obvious.[1] But even if, for the sake of argument, we accept the presumed superiority of rationing, the elementary theory of optimisation which underlies the so-called theory of 'planning' dictates that the government should allocate dollars between alternative uses such that the marginal dollar yields the same increase in social utility in any use. The Indian Government, however, appears to have allocated foreign exchange simply on the basis of giving a higher priority to its own foreign expenditures (categories G1, G2 and G3) than to private foreign expenditures (categories P1 and P2). That is to say, regardless of how much social utility might have been derived from a particular increase in private-sector imports, it would not be considered until after the government had met all its own expenditures abroad.[2]

Jagdish Bhagwati and T. N. Srinivasan put it as follows:

> 'The allocation of foreign exchange among alternative claimants and users in a direct control system . . . would presumably be with reference to a well-defined set of principles and criteria based on a system of priorities. In point of fact, however, there seem to have been few such criteria, if any, followed in practice.'[3]

With respect to imported inputs for private- and public-sector industries, a rule of 'essentiality' (that is, the input must be

---

[1] The classic argument for a free market is in M. Friedman, 'The case for flexible exchange rates', in his *Essays in Positive Economics*, University of Chicago Press, Chicago, 1953, pp. 157-203. Also V. S. Vartikar, *Commercial policy and economic development in India*, Praeger, New York, 1969, based on his PhD at Wayne State University; and D. Lal, *A liberal international economic order: the international monetary system and economic development*, Essays in International Finance No. 139, Princeton University, October 1980.

[2] An additive sub-utility function might be defined within each set of categories:

$$U_G = \sum_i \alpha_i . v_i(G_i) \qquad \alpha_1 > \alpha_2 > \alpha_3, \ \sum \alpha_i = 1$$

$$U_P = \sum_j \beta_j . w_j(P_j) \qquad \beta_1 > \beta_2 \qquad \sum \beta_j = 1 \ ;$$

where the $v_i(.)$ and the $w_j(.)$ are further sub-utility functions defined on each category, etc. None of these has ever been spelt out by the Indian Government, and certainly no amount of U_P has seemed substitutable for an iota of U_G.

[3] Bhagwati and Srinivasan, *op. cit.*, p. 38.

technically 'essential' to the production process) and a rule of 'indigenous availability' (that is, there must be absolutely no domestically-produced physical substitutes, regardless of cost and quality) seem to have been followed. But, as Bhagwati and Srinivasan report,

> '. . . the sheer weight of numbers made any meaningful listing of priorities extremely difficult. The problem was Orwellian: all industries had priority and how was each sponsoring authority to argue that some industries had more priority than others? It is not surprising, therefore, that the agencies involved in determining allocations by industry fell back on vague notions of "fairness", implying *pro rata* allocations with reference to capacity installed or employment, or shares defined by past import allocations or similar rules of thumb'.[1]

Clearly, in abjuring the free market and claiming a monopoly over foreign-exchange transactions, government planners have accepted certain premises as unquestionable: (a) that government-sponsored industrialisation is the best means to mass prosperity; (b) that a policy of indefinite import-substitution is the best means to industrialisation; and (c) that such a policy requires all foreign expenditures by government to take precedence over all private foreign expenditures. The trade and foreign-exchange policies pursued cannot be understood except by reference to domestic economic policies and, in particular, to the view held about the proper functions of government in and out of the market-place.

In addition to a plethora of controls, tariffs and outright bans on imports, there have been erratic policies, subsidising the export of 'new', non-traditional manufactures like engineering goods, and taxing – and even banning – the export of goods in which India has traditionally enjoyed a comparative advantage.[2]

---

[1] *Ibid.*, p. 38.

[2] In 1980, for example, exports of pig-iron and of sheep- and goat-meat were banned; an export duty on jute manufactures was imposed on 18 February and lifted on 8 September. (*Annual Report on Exchange Controls*, International Monetary Fund, 1981, pp. 205-13.) The *Import and Export Policy* (April 1982-March 1983) announced by the Commerce Ministry reported the banning of exports of cane, paraffin wax, mustard and rape-seed oil, and 'certain wild-life items', including lizards and robins.

[An embargo on the export of CTC (cut, tear and curl) tea was announced
[*Continued on p. 43*]

The over-valued rupee

Moreover, the rupee has been continuously over-valued. From 1949 to 1959, the official exchange rate of Rs. 4·76 to the US dollar was, on average, 12·3 per cent above the black-market rate, a figure which rose to 61 per cent between 1960 and 1965. From 1966 to 1970, the devalued official rate of Rs. 7·50 to the dollar was above the black-market rate by an average of 47·6 per cent, while from 1971 onwards the managed-peg rate has been above the black-market rate by an average of 24·3 per cent.[1]

Simple economics suggests that a free-market equilibrium rate would be somewhere between the black-market and official rates. An official exchange rate for the rupee fixed above that warranted by underlying relative demands for Indian and foreign goods, as well as by relative degrees of confidence in the rupee and the dollar, subsidises imports at the expense of exports. By discriminating in favour of its own foreign expenditures and against those of the private sector, the government has been the principal beneficiary of an over-valued rupee. If capital-intensive goods are the main imports and labour-intensive ones the main exports, an over-valued rupee further distorts incentives so as to favour the use of capital-intensive production processes over labour-intensive ones – in a country with a demonstrable abundance of relatively inexpensive labour!

With an eye to India, Krueger has argued the general issue in these terms:

'Subsidies can make any industry an export industry, even one that would not produce at all in an efficient allocation. Similarly, taxes can be levied on an industry that has comparative advantage which will penalise it enough to render domestic production entirely unprofitable. When taxes and subsidies are used, therefore, it is possible

[Continued from p. 42]
by the Ministry of Commerce on 24 December 1983. CTC is high-quality tea which accounts for about three-quarters of India's tea exports. The ban followed a doubling of domestic prices over the previous year, compulsory registration of tea dealers holding more than 1,000 kg. to prevent hoarding, and agreement by manufacturers to reduce their profit margins and cut prices of packaged tea by about 20 per cent (*Financial Times*, 14 December 1983). The Indian Government apparently feared that the supply of tea for the domestic market was going to run out (*The Times*, 5 January 1984). The effect of these measures is artificially to depress prices in the domestic market whilst raising them overseas (*The Economist*, 14 January 1984). – ED.]

[1] *Pick's Currency Yearbook*, various editions.

not only to distort the structure of production, but to distort it so much that the "wrong" commodities are exported.'[1]

The Indian Government's planners have had the idea of forcibly effecting a reversal in the comparative advantage of the country, as if by magic overnight. The hope might have been that a forced pace of industrialisation would somehow allow economies of scale to be reaped and thus soon make Indian industrial goods competitive enough in international markets to be the country's principal source of foreign exchange, displacing traditional manufactures like jute and textiles. In practice, however, as the evidence given by Bela Balassa and other economists demonstrates, such a policy has not succeeded to date and is most unlikely ever to do so.

India's import bill has risen continuously, most drastically after the 1973-74 quadrupling of petroleum prices; non-traditional manufactures have hardly been able to compete successfully in foreign markets; and the traditional exports of jute and textiles have suffered very severe setbacks. Balassa contrasts the consequences of the freer, outward-looking trade policies of South Korea, Singapore and Taiwan with those of the inward-looking, controlled régime of India as part of a study of 11 countries (including Argentina, Brazil, Colombia, Mexico, Chile, Israel and Yugoslavia) which, along with Hong Kong, account for most of the manufactured exports of developing countries. India's share of the total manufactured exports of these countries has fallen steadily from 65·4 per cent in 1953 to 50·7 per cent in 1960, to 31·2 per cent in 1966 and to a mere 10·3 per cent in 1973. The proportion exported of India's total manufactured output fell from 9·7 per cent in 1960 to 9·4 per cent in 1966 and to 8·6 per cent in 1973. In contrast, during the same two periods, the proportion of manufactured output exported rose from 1 to 14 to 41 per cent in South Korea, from 11 to 20 to 43 per cent in Singapore, and from 9 to 19 to 50 per cent in Taiwan.[2]

Balassa cogently argues that the adverse effects of a sudden change in external factors, such as the quadrupling of petroleum prices in 1973-74 or the 1974-75 Western recession, were absorbed much more easily by developing countries with large foreign-trade sectors than by those like India with relatively small ones:

[1] Krueger (1977), *op. cit.*, pp. 27-28.
[2] Balassa (1978), *op. cit.*, p. 39; Balassa (1980), *op. cit.*, p. 16.

[44]

'Outward orientation is associated with high export *and* import shares that permit reduction in non-essential imports without serious adverse effects on the functioning of the economy. By contrast, continued inward orientation involves limiting imports to an unavoidable minimum, so that any further reduction will impose a considerable cost in terms of growth. Furthermore, the greater flexibility of the national economies of countries pursuing an outward-oriented strategy, under which firms learn to live with foreign competition, makes it possible to change the product composition of exports in response to changes in world market conditions, whereas inward orientation entails establishing a more rigid economic structure.'[1]

In other words, if imports are both high in total value and diverse in composition, a rise in the relative price of a particular import for which home demand is relatively inelastic (like petroleum and its products) can be accommodated by a substitution of expenditure towards it and away from inessential imports for which demand is relatively elastic. A similar argument had typically been advanced by *advocates* of import-substitution when they maintained that the *exports* of a small country should be diverse and not concentrated on only a few goods since a decline in world prices would otherwise lead to serious falls in export revenues. This suggests that both critics and advocates of import-substitution might agree that, for a country which is a price-taker in world markets, the encouragement of a large foreign-trade sector is a way of diversifying the risk of adverse effects from changes in world prices. The question remains as to whether the positive theory of trade is correct in saying that the encouragement of comparative advantage is superior to import-substitution as a *means* of achieving a large foreign sector. From the contrasting experiences of, say, South Korea on the one hand and India on the other, the answer seems overwhelmingly to be that it is.

(iii) *Agriculture*

The Indian Government has instituted a multiple-pricing system for the major food-grains, especially rice and wheat. Farmers are compelled to sell a specified fraction of their output to the government, at a price fixed by the government which is significantly lower than that warranted by underlying supply and demand conditions. Farmers may sell the remainder of their output freely.

[1] *Ibid.*, p. 22.

The quantities the government acquires in this way, plus any it imports (imports being subsidised by the over-valuation of the exchange rate), are sold by ration at lower than free-market prices in the so-called 'fair-price' shops – which happen to be mainly in urban areas. Urban consumers may purchase part of their requirements from such shops and the remainder on the open market at higher prices. Astute middle-class urban housewives know that rationed grain is often of poorer quality than that sold on the open market. Accordingly, the former often constitutes part of the wages of the domestic servants of the urban household, while the family consumes the latter. Insofar as this is true, it suggests that farmers distinguish quality much better than do government officials, and that they use this advantage somewhat to partition their output into low- and high-quality, selling the first under compulsion to the government and the second on the open market.

While such is the general food policy of India, the compulsory procurement of grains and their distribution to the ration-shops is implemented by individual State governments and not by the Union Government. There have usually been numerous restrictions on inter-State movements of grain, so the States do not form a full customs-union; instead, the Union Government tries to be a central clearing-house, matching the desired imports of one State with the desired exports of another.[1]

Economic effects of ban on futures contracts

Furthermore, futures contracts in grains have been banned by law, in the belief that futures trading is conducive to speculation and that speculation is undesirable. A futures contract in grain consists simply of a promise by a seller to deliver an amount of grain to a buyer at some specified date in the future in return for payment at a price agreed today. The seller's incentive to enter into the contract is the guarantee of a certain sale, and the availability of funds now; the buyer's incentive is the guarantee of a certain price for future deliveries. The contract may be entered

---

[1] Short surveys of the relevant practices can be found in Lele, *op. cit.*, Appendix 1, pp. 225-37, and Sukhatme, *op. cit.*, pp. 29-37. Also Gilbert Brown, 'Agricultural pricing policies in developing countries', and G. E. Schuh, 'Approaches to "basic needs" and to "equity" that distort incentives in agriculture', in Schultz (ed.), *op. cit.*, pp. 84-113 and pp. 307-27 respectively.

[46]

into because buyer and seller have different expectations about what the spot price will be in the future. The buyer minimises his expected costs and the seller maximises his expected revenues; both are able to balance their budgets inter-temporally. Even if they have the *same* expectations about future spot prices, buyer and seller may still find it mutually profitable to enter into a futures contract as a way of insuring against risk. Forbidding such contracts by decree thus forces more risk onto both buyer and seller than they would normally be prepared to carry, and also induces them to balance their accounts in each period rather than inter-temporally. Alternative kinds of credit markets become relatively more lucrative, with the potential seller and buyer of futures wheat respectively borrowing and lending more than they would otherwise have done.[1]

The government has also expressed its determination to keep prices in ration-shops low. It has accordingly stockpiled large inventories of grain, apparently regardless of the costs of storage and spoilage or the alternative of holding larger foreign-exchange reserves to permit increased imports when necessary.

The ostensible, declared objective of all such policies has been to ensure that the poor do not suffer severe adverse income-effects from sudden rises in the price of food resulting (it has been thought) from the contingencies of rainfall and the actions of speculative traders. It is, however, an open secret that the policies have really been a means of (a) taxing farmers, who pay a smaller percentage of their income in direct and indirect taxes than do urban dwellers, and (b) subsidising urban consumers, who broadly comprise the industrial working class and the middle classes.

At the same time, however, the government and its advisers –

---

[1] Theoretical economists have long recognised that a fundamental flaw in, for example, the Arrow-Debreu model is its assumption that all conceivable futures contracts are practicable. The longest futures price actually quoted at the Chicago Board of Trade, however, would be for silver, at about two years; for grains, the longest would be only about three months. Since the natural market outcome is a far-cry from the theory, the Indian Government's fears about the effects of speculation appear to be much exaggerated.

To see the risk-dispersing character of a futures contract, let us suppose that both buyer and seller place a probability of one-half on prices being either 8 or 2; if they are risk-averse, they may prefer to trade at a certain futures price of 5 now, rather than wait for the future to unfold.

after the considerable hesitation recorded by David Hopper[1] – have also accepted that the best long-run prospects for increasing agricultural productivity lie in modernising traditional farming techniques. Given the outstanding results of the Green Revolution in wheat, they could hardly have arrived at any other conclusion. The problem from the government's point of view has been, as a sympathetic economist puts it,

'. . . how to procure a sufficient quantity of foodgrains at reasonable prices without jeopardising the farmers' incentives to produce more'.[2]

Thus, while taxing farmers *de facto* on their output, on the one hand, the government has tried, on the other, to promote the use of modern inputs by subsidising them both directly and through low-interest loans from the banks for such investment.

Distortions of incentives in agriculture

The distortions of efficient incentives caused by such policies are not difficult to see.

First, the low output prices of wheat and rice have, in effect, been discriminatory taxes on wheat and rice farmers. As Edward Schuh remarks, these discourage the production of '. . . the very crops that policy-makers believe the vulnerable groups should have greater access to . . .'.[3]

Vasant Sukhatme and Theodore Schultz have argued that, even between wheat and rice, there has been severe discrimination in favour of the former. At the official over-valued exchange rate, the price of domestic wheat has been significantly higher than imported, while at open-market rates for the rupee, the domestic price approximated the import price. For rice, however, the domestic price has been consistently *below* the import price. Sukhatme estimated that the deadweight loss in welfare from the underpricing of rice amounted to 8·5 per cent of total agricultural income in 1967-68 and to 2·2 per cent in 1970-71. He also calculated effective rates of protection, which were strongly negative for rice whether at official or open-market exchange rates and

[1] David Hopper, 'Distortions of agricultural development resulting from Government prohibitions', in Schultz (ed.), *op. cit.*, p. 69 ff.

[2] K. Prasad, 'Foodgrains policy 1966-1976', in Wadhwa (ed.), *op. cit.*, p. 479.

[3] Schultz (ed.), *op. cit.*, p. 309.

positive for wheat at the official exchange rate. Both he and Schultz conclude that the discrimination against rice has been a major factor in explaining the absence of a Green Revolution in rice on the scale of that in wheat.[1]

Secondly, the main beneficiaries of government subsidies for modern inputs have evidently been not the many small farmers but the fewer relatively large ones. As Gilbert Brown reports:

'Large-scale farmers buy most subsidised inputs. Poorer farmers usually lack the money to buy adequate amounts of fertiliser and pesticides, and are commonly unable to get credit except at near-prohibitive rates of often 60% to 100% per year. Even in countries with subsidised bank credit for agriculture, rich farmers get most of the credit because of legal or administrative restrictions and/or through open or disguised bribery. Credit and subsidy programmes for tractors, tube wells and other fixed investments also go mostly to the largest and richest farmers . . .

Water is also a subsidised input . . . The farmers who receive this subsidised water generally have substantially higher incomes (because of the water) than farmers without access to public irrigation. Thus, claims that water should be subsidised to help small farmers misses the point that most farmers with irrigation have higher incomes than those who do not.'[2]

Brown argues that subsidies for inputs have been made necessary only to offset the forced depression of output prices. Moreover, the social benefit from subsidising inputs is limited to when the input is first introduced:

'Once the benefits and technique of using the input are widely known, however, the continuation of such subsidies serves largely to increase the benefit-cost ratio of using the input . . .'.

Whether it is better to continue with artificially low input and output prices or to adjust towards a free market in both must take into account that the subsidies have encouraged more capital-intensity in production, and also that the

'. . . low prices of certain inputs, particularly water, are often associated with widespread waste and inefficient use of the resource'.[3]

[1] Sukhatme, *op. cit.*, pp. 74-86; T. W. Schultz, 'On the economics and politics of agriculture', in Schultz (ed.), *op. cit.*, p. 15 ff.
[2] Schultz (ed.), *op. cit.*, pp. 92-93. [3] *Ibid.*, p. 95.

Thirdly, the farmer who is too small to find investment in storage facilities profitable may also consider it not worth his while to hold any of his output for sale on the open market. He will then sell it all to the government – at a below-market price.

A general conclusion would seem to be that, if the combined effect of input subsidies and forced grain sales to government has been a net subsidy to agriculture, then it has been a progressive subsidy; whereas if the combined effect has been a net tax on agriculture, then it has been a regressive tax. The Marxists may be quite right to protest that what gains there have been in agriculture have accrued to the relatively larger farmers, while smaller peasants and farmers are becoming landless labourers in growing numbers as a result of bankruptcy (that is, there has been increasing 'rural proletarianisation', to use the Marxists' picturesque phrase). But if this is true, the cause can be traced unambiguously to the Indian Government's belief – vociferously shared by the Marxists – that the way towards the declared objective of helping the poor is by extensive interference in the price system. Besides, the industrial working class demonstrably benefits from low food prices, so the honest Marxist must face up to being torn by divided loyalties between the rural and the urban proletariats.

Srinivasan put it as follows in a 1974 survey article:

'The public distribution system with respect to foodgrains . . . operated to the benefit of *all* those living in metropolitan cities and other large urban concentrations while *all others*, including rich and poor in relatively small urban and almost all rural areas, did not benefit at all. When one recalls that the rural population includes the most abject among the poor, namely landless workers, the inequity of the system becomes glaring. And in urban areas, the existence of the system and the fact that the ration is often inadequate provides incentives for a household to falsify the data on its size and age-composition given to the rationing authorities, as well as to create bogus or ghost ration-cards, not to speak of the corruption of the personnel manning the rationing administration.'[1]

Statism in Indian agriculture – a British legacy?

The history of the extensive control of agriculture – which has

---

[1] T. N. Srinivasan, 'Income Distribution: A survey of policy-aspects', in Wadhwa (ed.), *op. cit.*, p. 265. That the small farmer may not find it profitable to invest in storage, and that (if it has been taxed) agriculture has been taxed regressively, are also remarked upon by Srinivasan.

included a partial government monopsony, forcibly-depressed output prices, inter-State restrictions on grain movements, and urban ration-shops – can be traced to the last years of British rule, as an attempt to bolster the popularity of the imperial régime.[1] The continuation and reinforcement of statism in agriculture in independent India has evidently rested on certain premises, namely, that the private market would be grossly inefficient and would be dominated by a few traders continually reaping large speculative profits, with both the small farmer and the ordinary consumer suffering in consequence.

Uma Lele's fine study of the private grain trade, however, shows the real picture to be quite different. She found that the trade was highly competitive, that individual traders were rational agents (given the constraints of technology and government policy), that locational price differences closely reflected transport costs, and that temporal price differences closely reflected storage costs. She argued that, while there was considerable scope for government activity, it should be in the form, not of interfering in the competitive market, but rather of *encouraging* the market to work – by, for example, disseminating relevant information such as crop forecasts, standardising weights and measures, constructing or improving roads and encouraging efficiency in the market for the transport of grain, etc.[2]

The evident neglect of such findings as these, and the continued application of policies inimical to competition and the free market, suggest that successive governments of independent India have been hardly more concerned for the rural poor – whether as farmer or consumer – and hardly less concerned with bolstering their popularity in the urban areas than were the British.

(iv) *Employment*

An obvious consequence of the economic policies described above has been the distortion of the individual citizen's calculation of the expected benefits and costs of living and working in urban areas compared with the rural countryside. The forced depression

[1] Lele, *op. cit.*, p. 2, where reference is made to Sir Henry Knight, *Food-Administration in India*, Stanford University Press, Stanford, 1954.

[2] Lele, *op. cit.*, pp. 214-24.

of output prices in agriculture and the plethora of foreign-trade policies which discriminate against agriculture certainly seem to have artificially depressed the expected incomes of farmers. At the same time, a large 'public sector' in industry, *plus* the array of foreign-trade policies which have protected private industry, *plus* the indirect subsidisation of food sold in urban ration-shops certainly seem to have artificially raised expected urban incomes. Predictably, the reaction has been a vast and continuing net migration from the villages to the towns and cities, even after adjusting for the seasonal nature of agriculture. This drift has been the subject of much inquiry and discussion by development economists.[1] I propose to set it aside and examine instead a different aspect of employment policy which has not received nearly as much attention, namely, the consequences of putting into effect the clauses in the 1950 Indian Constitution mentioned above (p. 31) which authorised discrimination in employment and public education in favour of the 'Scheduled' castes and tribes, as well as other policies which discriminate on grounds of ethnic origin.

Ethnic problems similar to USA

The consequences have been similar in several respects to those in America of 'affirmative action' towards so-called 'racial minorities', and it will be useful to draw out the analogy a little.

As Thomas Sowell has cogently argued in recent years, the racial composition of contemporary American society is a complex mosaic, and no-one can say with certainty how it has come to be what it is today. In such circumstances, for the government to try to isolate a single contingent characteristic like 'race', partition society on the basis of census data according to this characteristic, and then construct public policies accordingly, is to introduce an enormous arbitrariness into economic life. By merely defining a group by reference to a single contingent characteristic which

[1] For example, M. Todaro, 'A model of labor migration and urban unemployment in less developed countries', *American Economic Review*, March 1969, 59, pp. 138-48; J. P. Harris & M. Todaro, 'Migration, unemployment and development: a two-sector analysis', *American Economic Review*, March 1970, 60, pp. 126-42. The best paper known to the author is by Jerome Rothenberg, 'On the economics of internal migration', Working Paper No. 189, Dept. of Economics, MIT, July 1976.

all its members seem to possess, the intrinsic complexity of the individual person is lost or overlooked. Two members of the same race may be very different from each other in every relevant characteristic (income, education, political preference, and so on), and indeed resemble members of other races more closely in them. A policy which introduces a citizen's race as a relevant factor in the assignment of jobs or college places partitions the citizenry into vague groups: members of groups who *are* very different from members of other groups in characteristics *other* than race rarely competing with each other anyway, while the burden and beneficence of the state's policies fall on members of groups who are *not* very different from members of other groups in characteristics other than race:

'. . . costs are borne disproportionately by those members of the general population who meet those standards with the least margin and are therefore most likely to be the ones displaced to make room for minority applicants. Those who meet the standards by the widest margin are not directly affected – that is, pay no costs. They are hired, admitted or promoted as if blacks did not exist. People from families with the most general ability to pay also have the most ability to pay for the kind of education and training that makes such performance possible. The costs of special standards are paid by those who do not. Among the black population, those most likely to benefit from the lower standards are those closest to meeting the normal standards. It is essentially an implicit transfer of wealth among people least different in non-racial characteristics. For the white population it is a regressively graduated tax in kind, imposed on those who are rising but not on those already on top.'[1]

At the same time, there is, in effect, a progressively graduated subsidy for members of the 'minority' group in favour of those who are already closest to meeting the general standards. Those in the mainstream of each group are largely unaffected; it is at the margins of competition that the bitterness caused by such policies will be felt and will manifest itself.

It would seem that the situation in India – where the racial mosaic is if anything more complex than in America – is somewhat analogous. In recent years there has been civil tension and violence in the streets as poor Muslims, 'caste' Hindus, Sikhs and others

---

[1] Thomas Sowell, *Knowledge and Decisions*, Basic Books, New York, 1980, pp. 268-69.

have protested at being edged out of jobs and promotions by equally poor, or wealthier, members of the 'Scheduled Castes'. In March-April 1981, for instance, there was widespread civil tension and violence in Gujarat over the reservation of places in the State's medical colleges. A quarter of these places were statutorily reserved for members of the 'Scheduled Castes', with any not taken up by qualified candidates from these groups accruing to them in the future, thereby rapidly excluding from general competition as many as half the total number of places.[1]

The cruel paradox is that, while the position of many members (perhaps the vast majority) of the 'Scheduled Castes' *vis-à-vis* 'caste' Hindus remains one of degradation and persecution – quite regardless of the constitutional guarantees of *equality* in the eyes of the law – the relatively few who have succeeded in taking advantage of the discriminatory statutes have aroused the indignation of those who have not – causing even more animosity towards the 'Scheduled Castes' in general. One commentator observes the emergence of a 'new elite' among the 'Scheduled Castes' which 'ceases to identify with its caste brethren'; while, at the same time, the law on equality 'is so widely flouted precisely because the Scheduled Castes have not the means or courage to seek its protection . . .' He concludes:

> 'Contrived gestures such as are now popular will either not benefit [the Scheduled Castes] . . . or will do so only by further lowering already deplorable academic and administrative standards'.[2]

Moreover, when all government posts are advertised with a caveat that 10 or 15 per cent of them are reserved for members of the 'Scheduled Castes' and 'Scheduled Tribes', there is a considerable incentive for people to persuade Parliament to declare them as being such. And that also has happened.

Discrimination in employment on the ground of caste has not been the only kind of discrimination practised by the Indian state. In what may be the most thorough study currently available on the origins, consequences and legal history of official discrimination in India, Weiner, Katzenstein and Rao have described the

---

[1] 'The logic of protection', *The Statesman*, Editorial, 19 March 1981; also the Editorial, 'Danger of caste war', 27 February 1981.

[2] S. K. Datta Ray, 'Backlash to protection: fancy gifts ignore real reform', *The Statesman Weekly*, 21 March 1981.

plethora of policies pursued by the central and state governments which have used not caste but ethnic origin as a criterion for public employment (with the private sector also often being 'encouraged' to follow suit):

> 'Preferences are given to those who belong to the "local" community, with "local" understood as referring to the numerically dominant linguistic group in the locality.'[1]

The authors conclude that what is emerging in India is

> '. . . a government-regulated labour market in which various ethnic groups are given a reserved share of that market. Competition for employment is thus not among all Indians, but within specified linguistic, caste, and tribal groups.

> '. . . various ethnic groups, therefore, fight politically for a share of that labour market. The major political struggles are often over who should get reservations, how the boundaries of the ethnic groups should be defined, and how large their share should be. There are also political struggles over whether there should be reservations in both education and employment, in private as well as in public employment, and in promotions as well as hiring. The preferential policies themselves have thus stimulated various ethnic groups to assert their "rights" to reservations.'[2]

Economic case against discrimination

It is not difficult to understand the general economic argument against discrimination on grounds such as caste or ethnic origin. If a private employer indulges a personal preference to hire only people of an ethnic kind A when there are more able or better-qualified candidates of other ethnic kinds $B, C, D, \ldots$, available, and if the product of his firm is subject to competition in the market from other enterprises which do not discriminate on criteria which are irrelevant to economic efficiency, we may confidently expect the discriminating employer's product to become uncompetitive and his profits to fall. The best and most obvious example of this would be in the professional sports industry in the USA: a

[1] M. Weiner, M. F. Katzenstein, K.V.N. Rao, *India's preferential policies: migrants, the middle classes and ethnic equality*, University of Chicago Press, Chicago, 1981, pp. 16-17.

[2] *Ibid.*, p. 5.

'whites-only' basketball or football team would be immediately vanquished on the games-field into bankruptcy.

If government pursues employment policies which discriminate according to economically irrational criteria such as caste or ethnic origin, or if it forces all private firms to do likewise, there will certainly be inefficiency resulting in a loss of real aggregate output in the economy. In the terms of modern economics, a vector of total outputs which would be feasible given the parameters of the economy, and which would leave everyone either better off or at least no worse off, would not be achieved.

In sum, the consequence of direct and widespread government interference in the labour market in India appears to have been, not only a disregard for the principle of equality before the law for every citizen (in a nascent republic of immensely diverse peoples), but also a loss of real output and an enormous 'politicisation' of economic life whereby individual success becomes increasingly tied to political power and increasingly removed from personal merit, enterprise and effort. In addition, the composition of occupations in the economy has been indirectly distorted by the set of industrial, agricultural and foreign-trade policies pursued by successive governments.

6. THE MALFUNCTIONING OF GOVERNMENT

IT MIGHT be thought that a large and flabby 'public sector' in industry and commerce, labyrinthine controls on private industry, a government monopoly of foreign-exchange dealings, the over-valuation of the currency, indefinite import-substitution, forcibly depressed output and input prices in agriculture, enormous politicisation of the labour market, disregard for equality before the law, and distortion of the composition of occupations would constitute a sufficient catalogue of symptoms of grave illness in the political economy of a nation. Sadly, however, there are in modern India other symptoms too which I can mention only briefly here.

An opinion frequently encountered among urban Indians (as well as among the majority of Western development economists) is that government control over the size of the population is a necessary condition for economic development, and indeed that it is the failure of government to do this that has dissipated the economic growth that would otherwise have resulted from the economic policies pursued. The urban Indian witnesses the hovels and shanty-towns inhabited by migrant families from the country-side attracted by the policies discussed previously, and he experiences the resulting congestion. So does the Western development economist when he ventures out of his hotel into the city streets. Very often, that is his only personal experience of the legendary 'poor masses' of India. It is understandable that such princely discomfiture should lead him to the opinion that the poor are mindless in their breeding habits and that they must be persuaded, bullied or compelled to change. If this opinion were true, it would seem to point to a neat and simple solution to many of the woes of poor countries, and India in particular. But if the opinion is false and yet widely believed, it would cause governments to be, as it were, barking up the wrong tree.

Is population control desirable?

It is, however, far from established, and certainly not at all obvious, that demographic control is either necessary or desirable in India or elsewhere. In the first place, when the rate of infant mortality is known and experienced by rural people to be high, there will be more births than there would have been otherwise. Secondly, it is perfectly clear that children are an investment good in traditional societies such as those of rural India. Even young children are a source of family income, either directly by working outside the home or indirectly by working at domestic chores and thereby releasing adult members of the family for outside work. For a child to be absent from primary school or to drop out within a few years is not necessarily truancy; it may be the outcome of a rational economic calculation about where his time may be better spent towards increasing the household's income. Furthermore, in traditional societies adult children are the principal source of support for elderly and retired parents.

To know of the existence of artificial measures of contraception certainly enlarges the alternatives open to a couple. Assuming that such knowledge is not in itself a cause of unhappiness (as it can be if there are conflicting religious commitments), a couple may

[57]

certainly be better off with that knowledge because of their ability to control the number and timing of their children. The couple might also have fewer children – though there is no necessary or causal connection between a knowledge of contraception and the number of children born to a couple. Rational calculation may produce the same number of children as the caprice of nature, the implication being that in general there is no causal connection between the availability of contraceptives and the rate of growth of the population. The value of a public policy which encourages the use of artificial contraception is not so much that it reduces the number of births as that it may allow couples more control over their own lives. Whether or not artificial contraception should be publicly subsidised is quite another question.

The Indian Government has expended considerable resources in propagating and subsidising artificial birth control. The results appear to have been, at best, indifferent (coupled as birth control has been with indirect incentives for large families) and, at worst, cruel – as when frenetic zeal spilled over into demands for, and the implementation of, compulsory sterilisation. For this author, however, the important consideration would seem to be not so much the exact costs and benefits of the demographic policies pursued as the critical acknowledgement that they have little or nothing to do with the fundamental causes of mass economic development.[1]

It remains a stark paradox that, with a general literacy rate of perhaps 30 per cent, India still produces the third largest absolute number of science and engineering graduates in the world. This reflects the lopsidedness of the educational system, continued from British times, in which higher education is enormously subsidised relative to primary education. In addition, entry into the civil services requires a college or university education, which in turn requires a good private secondary school education, which in turn requires a good preparatory school education. Strenuously competing to enter prep. school, with the help of outside tutoring,

[1] P. T. Bauer, 'Population explosion: myths and realities', in *Equality, the Third World and Economic Delusion*, Harvard University Press, Cambridge, Mass., 1981, pp. 42-65, contains some of the clearest arguments known to the author about this question; also M. Weiner, *India at the Polls: the Parliamentary Election of 1977*, American Enterprise Institute, Washington DC, 1978, pp. 35-39.

is the unhappy fate of many a five- or six-year-old in the towns and cities, followed by strenuous competition in secondary school, college and university, and finally at the doorstep of government (or a foreign university).

A job in government – any job in government – has carried prestige since Mughal times. In addition to the prestige and the obvious benefits of tenure where other 'decent' jobs are scarce, there has been in recent times the inner satisfaction from a belief that a person can truly do his best for his country only by being in government. Tens of thousands of youths spend significant personal resources (such as whole years in cramming schools) to compete for a few annual openings in government. It is only to be expected that the competent, ambitious, patriotic youth who succeeds will mature into a respected mandarin with an unshakeable conviction in the good his government has done for the masses, and in the further good yet in prospect.

Failure to anticipate monsoon damage and disarray of the judicial system

The most serious examples of the malfunctioning of civil government in India are probably the failure to take feasible public precautions against the monsoons and the disarray of the judicial system. Official estimates, for instance, of the damage caused by flooding to homes, crops and public utilities in a few weeks of July-August 1981 alone amounted to over Rs 1 billion, with 10·8 million people 'affected', 35,000 head of cattle lost, and 195,000 homes damaged. The full magnitude of the devastation which annually visits vast areas can be understood perhaps only by those in rural India, although the towns and cities also regularly suffer considerable chaos.[1]

As for the disarray of the judicial system, *The Statesman* lamented in July 1980:

'The simplest matter takes an inordinate amount of time, remedies seldom being available to those without means or influence. Of the more than 16,000 cases pending in the Supreme Court, about 5,000 were introduced more than five years ago; while nearly 16,000 of the

[1] '10·8 million people affected by floods', *The Statesman Weekly*, 22 August 1981; also 'Down the drain', Editorial in *The Statesman*, 8 July 1981.

backlog of more than 600,000 cases in our high courts have been hanging fire for over a decade. Allahabad is the worst offender but there are about 75,000 uncleared cases in the Calcutta High Court in addition to well over a million in West Bengal's lower courts . . .'[1]

Such a state of affairs has been caused not only by lazy and corrupt policemen, court clerks and lawyers, but also by the paucity of judges and magistrates. In addition, however,

'. . . a vast volume of laws provokes endless litigation as much because of poor drafting which leads to disputes over interpretation as because they appear to violate particular rights and privileges. Land legislation offers an example of radical zeal running away with legal good sense, giving rise to thousands of suits against the Government . . .'[1]

When governments determinedly do what they need not or should not do, it may be expected that they will fail to do what civil government positively should be doing. In a sentence, that has been the tragedy of modern India.

Part IV: Reform

7. A LIBERAL AGENDA

IT WILL by now have become evident to the reader from the descriptions and arguments given above that, in the judgement of the present author, only a set of radical changes in policy can put the Indian economy on a path to higher mass prosperity within a free and healthy body politic. I shall therefore put forward a tentative manifesto for reform, adding some predictions about which classes of citizens would be most likely to support or oppose a particular proposal.

The scope and intention of such a manifesto should be made clear at the outset. As Aristotle taught, a set of actions which are the means towards certain ends may themselves be the ends

---

[1] 'Justice with speed', Editorial in *The Statesman*, Calcutta and New Delhi, 21 July 1980.

towards which other prior means have to be taken.[1] The ultimate ends of economic advice in India are to seek to bring about mass prosperity under conditions of individual freedom. The proposals which follow are to be construed as means towards those ultimate ends. But they also constitute a set of intermediate ends, and their implementation would require further judgement about the best prior means towards achieving them. In economic policy, for instance, a firm but gradual phasing-in over a period of three or four years may be the best way to minimise the hardships entailed by the adjustment. For reasons which will become clear, however, I shall not here try to answer the question as to how the proposals might best be implemented.

(a) *Effects of foreign policy on the domestic economy*

It will be useful to begin with a short and very incomplete consideration of foreign policy insofar as it may bear upon domestic economic policies. It is a settled fact of international politics that, while there is no obvious connection between a nation's economic and political institutions and the choice of strategic allies it faces, people's subjective perceptions and opinions of the social arrangements in a foreign country can be deeply influenced by whether that country is seen as a potential ally or adversary. A related and equally settled fact is that war, or the fear of war, can make for the most incongruous of bed-fellows.

In contemporary India, it is quite evident that the antipathy and pessimism towards market institutions found among the urban public, and the sympathy and optimism to be found for collectivist or statist ones, has been caused to a very significant extent by the perception that the United States is relatively hostile towards India while the Soviet Union is relatively friendly. This was not always so. The official affection between the United States and India in the early years of the Republic was grounded in sincerity and goodwill. The roots of its demise are probably to be found in the split between the Soviet Union and China in the late 1950s which, in a short period of time, made the latter a valuable strategic ally for the United States against the former. By the early 1970s, the spectre of a joint military threat to India from a totalitarian China and a militarist Pakistan – and especially

[1] Aristotle, *op. cit.*, 1,094a1–1,094b11.

a threat which it was perceived democratic America would do little or nothing to thwart – made it prudent for democratic India to become the virtual ally of totalitarian Russia.

Such a configuration on the international chess-board need not have been detrimental to India's economic development. It is possible to imagine a liberal state allied to a totalitarian one for strategic reasons, yet maintaining liberal economic policies domestically and internationally. In practice,[1] however, the extent of 'economic collaboration', bilateral trading arrangements, 'joint ventures', barter agreements, 'cultural exchanges', and the like into which the Indian Government has entered with the Soviet bloc, appears significantly to exceed what it has achieved with the Western powers. In particular, Soviet arms have in recent years been purchased more often and then manufactured under licence. This too need not have been economically detrimental if the Soviet products had in practice been competitive on international markets in terms of price and quality. As is common knowledge, however, this is often not so. It therefore appears that part of the price India has had to pay for the strategic support of the Soviet Union has been the foisting on her of low-quality, high-priced Soviet goods, whether arms or steel mills or technical know-how. At the same time, for reasons which are partly historical and partly related to these considerations, direct foreign investment by private Western firms has been treated with, at best, coolness and, at worst, open hostility.

A change in India's foreign policy

If the economic liberalisation that will be proposed here for India is to be effective, a truly independent yet prudent foreign policy may be required to accompany it. A change in the present strategic configuration – in which the United States is perceived in India to be virtually the ally of both China and Pakistan, while India is perceived in the United States to be virtually the ally of the Soviet Union – is unlikely until and unless the United States finds it in her best interests in the region to distance herself from China and Pakistan, which is unlikely to happen without a *rap-*

[1] There are few thorough studies known to the author that are relevant. One such is Asha L. Dattar, *India's Economic Relations with the USSR and Eastern Europe 1953-1969*, Cambridge University Press, Cambridge, 1972.

prochement between the Soviet Union and China. A drastic alternative way for India to reduce her dependence upon the Soviet Union would be the kind of divorce Egypt effected some years ago, followed by an alliance with the Western powers. This might, however, undermine once more the independence of foreign policy and be perceived in India as a move from the devil to the deep sea.

The prudent remaining alternative would appear to be an earnest and vigorous pursuit of serious no-war pacts with Pakistan and China, combined with an appropriately small independent nuclear deterrent. It seems to the author that the reasons which commend this course are closely analogous to those offered by the present American and British governments for pursuing serious no-war negotiations with the Soviet bloc whilst simultaneously improving the Western nuclear deterrent.

(b) *Liberalisation of foreign trade*

Not only would the truly independent foreign policy proposed in the preceding paragraph allow India to distance herself from the Soviet Union; it would probably also prompt the Western powers to end the intergovernmental transfers which go by the name of 'foreign aid'. For reasons that Peter Bauer has emphasised over many years, an end to such transfers might be a boon in disguise for India.[1] In particular, it would require the government to seek to balance the foreign-exchange accounts without becoming obligated to the Western powers, and this in turn would require a major economic transformation from a closed and protectionist economy to an open one which harnessed India's comparative advantages.

An initial liberalisation of foreign trade, involving a transition from quotas to tariffs, would probably be supported by private industry as a whole. It would, however, be opposed by incumbent politicians and government officials since it would dissipate the rents they receive under the closed régime. A subsequent reduction in tariffs, a withdrawal of export subsidies, and the free floating of the rupee would be opposed by those private firms (and their labour unions) which would be uncompetitive internationally – probably those in 'non-traditional' industries. The

[1] Bauer (1981), *op. cit.*, Chapters 5 & 6.

[63]

measures would, however, be supported by ordinary consumers, by private firms in traditional industries like jute manufactures and textiles, and particularly by farmers.

Once private industry became subject to the strict discipline of international competition again, there would be no reason whatsoever for government-imposed internal controls which were not conducive to free and fair competition among firms for the consumer's rupee. The repeal of the plethora of licensing policies would dissipate the large rents attached to the controls under the present régime. Since these rents are paid by private industry and received, directly or indirectly, by incumbent politicians and government officials, the former could be expected to welcome repeal and the latter to oppose it vigorously.

(c) *Privatisation of 'public-sector' industries*

At the same time, for the so-called 'public-sector' industries to face international competition, when they are currently monopolists or oligopolists, would demand such an improvement in economic discipline as probably to require the shares of most of them to be sold on the open market, with marginal-cost pricing imposed on the remainder. There is no economic reason why the Government of India should be engaged in commercial or merchant banking and insurance, or in industries from steel, machine-tools, ship-building and fertilisers to wrist-watches, hotels and beer. Nor is there any cogent reason why it should be a major producer, let alone a monopolist, in the road, rail, air and sea transport industries. Large-scale privatisation would be supported by private citizens in general, and would also draw out the reputedly vast private funds which circulate in the untaxable underground economy. But such measures would probably be opposed vigorously by the government officials who currently manage these industries, as well as by the public-sector labour unions.

(d) *Free-market pricing in agriculture*

With the repudiation of the mistaken premise that government-sponsored industrialisation is the best means to mass economic development, the free-market pricing of agricultural outputs and

[64]

the removal of all controls that are not conducive to free competition among farmers should follow. This would be welcomed by all farmers and perhaps by the rural population in general. It could also be expected to provide much encouragement to the technological transformation of traditional agriculture. The abolition of ration-shops in urban areas would be opposed by the industrial working class, by the urban middle classes in general, and by government officials and employees engaged in the present régime of public distribution. Further, farmers, especially relatively large ones, might be expected to oppose the concomitant free-market pricing of agricultural inputs, including credit and fertilisers, as would those government employees presently charged with distributing these inputs.

The ending of the distortions in agricultural output and input prices would establish a conclusive case for uniform systems of taxation in the economy, and especially for income from agriculture to be treated on a par with income from other occupations. These systems could locally include direct subsidies to those (whether in rural or urban areas) who are unable to provide any income for themselves, such as the insane and the severely disabled – all of whom are currently cared for, if at all, by private charity, and none of whom, strangely enough, appears to enter the moral calculations of socialist and Marxist economists.

(e) *Tax revenues for public goods*

The first and most important destination of tax revenues, whether raised centrally, provincially or locally, must be the provision of public goods – central, provincial and local. In an earlier section (pp. 17-21) we have seen what kinds of goods these should be. Among the most urgent in India are more effective precautions against the monsoons and improvements in the efficiency of the systems of civil and criminal justice. The former might include measures to prevent soil erosion and the building of better dams, embankments, canals and roads. Such programmes would be likely to command practically unanimous support in the localities in which they were implemented.

Reforms of the judicial system might include raising the salaries of judges and policemen, as well as the penalties for their misconduct; improving the training and morale of the police, with the object of increasing public confidence in them (especially in the villages); and expanding the number of courts, at least temporarily until the monumental backlog of cases has been reduced and brought under control. A general reduction in the political and administrative direction of economic life would lead to fewer law suits being brought against the government itself, and thus provide further relief for the judiciary. Widespread prison reform may also be required if the reports are true that a large proportion of those held prisoner for a number of years have yet to be brought to trial, and that potential prosecution witnesses, if they are poor and uneducated, are themselves sometimes kept in gaol until a case comes to court. Such reforms would command the support of everyone except criminals, capricious litigants and corrupt or incompetent members of the police and judiciary, none of which groups, it must be supposed, comprises a political constituency.

Together with improvements in the system of justice, the principle of equality before the law would have to be taken seriously. This would require the dispensation of justice by the state to be, as it were, a process blind to the infinitely diverse caste and ethnic characteristics of the citizenry, which in turn would imply the repeal of all laws – whether central, provincial or local – permitting governmental authorities to discriminate in favour of a particular politically-specified caste or ethnic group. Merely to have written 'equality before the law' into the Constitution without really believing it either possible or desirable is to allow the mutual caste and ethnic bigotry of private citizens to be exploited for political ends. That innumerable members of a caste, or religious or ethnic community have suffered at the hands of another, and that members of the 'Scheduled Castes' in particular have been victims of enormous cruelty, should not prevent acknowledgement of the sober fact that the past is irretrievable, or that it is similar cruelty in the present and future against any citizen at the hands of any other, or the state, that the declaration of Fundamental Rights was intended to prevent.

(f) *Other reforms*

Other proposals could also be suggested: the introduction of vouchers for primary and secondary education; a serious assessment

[66]

of the benefits from and costs of subsidies to higher education; an end to the government monopoly of radio and television; a revision of government pay-scales to make them competitive with the private sector, together with equivalent reductions in non-pecuniary benefits; a de-centralisation of public spending decisions from New Delhi to the State capitals and from there to the districts; and so on. However, it is hardly necessary to go further, since even a limited liberal agenda would appear doomed to be still-born.

Incumbent politicians, government officials, and the public-sector unions in general would vigorously oppose any reduction in government intervention in the economy for fear of losing the rents and sinecures of the *status quo*. Indeed, professional politicians in general could be expected to be averse to any lessening of the politicisation of economic life.

In other countries, a political party proposing such a reduction in government intervention would usually enjoy the backing of private industry. In India, however, private industry in general would probably see it in its own interest to support only the reduction of *internal* controls, whilst vigorously opposing reductions in the neo-mercantilist *external* controls. In July 1981, for example, I asked a prominent industrialist to imagine first a free-market régime at home: 'That would be very welcome indeed', he replied enthusiastically. I then asked him to imagine a policy of free trade: 'That would wipe us out', he replied gravely. His answers indicate very well what is perhaps the single most important feature of the equilibrium that has emerged in India: by accepting without significant protest the constraints and costs imposed upon it by the government and its 'planners', *the private corporate sector has traded the freedom of enterprise for mercantilist monopoly profits in the home market.*

When Indian Marxists rail about collusion between the 'national bourgeoisie' (that is, the governmental class) and the 'comprador bourgeoisie' (that is, the private sector), they make a cogent point as old as Adam Smith's critique of mercantilism.[1] But, again, they fail to see that the fortunes of the industrial working-class have also risen with those of the private and public industries that have gained from the present régime. Moreover, a large proportion of industrial workers and blue-collar government em-

---

[1] Adam Smith, *op. cit.*, Book IV; also B. Baysinger *et al.*, 'Mercantilism as a rent-seeking society', in Buchanan *et al.* (eds.), *op. cit.*, pp. 235-68.

ployees are migrants with families left behind in rural areas; these rural families might also oppose reductions in the transfers currently received by their migrant relatives. Finally, while joining other farmers in welcoming a free market in grain, the politically influential larger farmers could be expected to oppose the direct taxation of agricultural incomes and the elimination of subsidies for inputs.

Who is left who would gain from the kinds of reforms proposed here? Only the ordinary citizen *qua* consumer, the rural poor and the residuum of severely disabled citizens unable to create any income for themselves. None of these has been or is likely to become an effective political force.

India's 'unhappy equilibrium'

The economy of the first Indian Republic has tended towards a broad and increasingly unhappy equilibrium. Distortions of efficient relative prices and wages lead to both substitution and income effects. Those who lose from one distortion rationally seek another from which they may gain; those who lose from the second seek a third; and so on *ad infinitum* until a maze of distorted incentives are in place and a host of income transfers are in progress – sometimes offsetting losses, sometimes not. Tullock has emphasised that the problem is not only that there are deadweight losses in welfare, but also that people are led '. . . to employ resources in attempting to obtain or prevent such transfers'.[1] In modern India, the waste of productive resources put to the pursuit of such transfers has been incalculable. The reforms proposed here would cut through the maze of distorted incentives and institutions all at once – for which very reason it seems unlikely they can come to be implemented.

The economic significance of a political attitude of individualism is that it clearly recognises the relationship between individual effort and reward, and the relationship between cause and consequence generally. An attitude of statism obscures or obliterates this relationship. In republican India, statism has pervaded all public discourse and prompted most public policy. Successive groups of politicians and government officials seem never to have recognised the fundamental nature of those functions of govern-

[1] G. Tullock in Buchanan *et al.* (eds.), *op. cit.*, p. 48.

ment which are the indispensable prerequisites of civil peace and mass prosperity. Nor have they understood that it is no part of government's agenda to be the driving force to mass prosperity, and that this can come (if it will) only from innumerable individual efforts in the pursuit of private rewards.

This is not at all to say that those in government have been ill-intentioned. On the contrary, they may have sincerely sought the public good whilst introducing a leviathan government into the market-place and neglecting the proper duties of government outside it. As Bauer has remarked in a related context:

'Their financial benefits may appear to be fortuitous, as if Adam Smith's invisible hand were to work in reverse, so that those who sought the public good achieve what was no part of their intention, namely personal prosperity.'[1]

It is indeed possible that the basic fact of human nature that individual households everywhere ordinarily know most about, and are only concerned with, their own well-being has never been acknowledged in modern India. The simple secret of a stable and prosperous polity is to create institutions which *harness* the universal pursuit of individual self-interest, and not ones which pretend that men are selfless saints. A polity where this fact is acknowledged would not have to depend for the viability of its institutions on mere exhortation, as the institutions of the Indian Republic seem perpetually fated to do, even while the competitive pursuit of self-interest is everywhere manifest.

The logic of economic reasoning and the adducement of economic evidence have in the past had little effect in India because the distribution of gains and losses from the policies pursued has been closely matched by the distribution of effective political power. This distribution seems most likely to continue, and so the prospects of significant and sustained endogenous reform seem, to this author at least, very small. Changes in external constraints seem to be the only likely source of a major disturbance to the equilibrium, and there can be no guarantee that the results will be for the better. This is a sad and troubling conclusion to come to, for a citizen of India or anyone else who has loved the country. It places this author in the paradoxical position of believing his arguments to be broadly correct – while hoping they are not.

[1] Bauer (1981), *op. cit.*, p. 144.

Some IEA Titles on 'Development Economics'

Hobart Paperback 16
THE POVERTY OF 'DEVELOPMENT ECONOMICS'
Deepak Lal   1983   £3·00

'... written by the distinguished Indian economist Deepak Lal ... [it] should be compulsory reading for the advocates of the New International Economic Order, the protectionists, the autarkists and the admirers of the Brandt Report. ... Lal argues that the vogue for development economics ... originated from a widespread but ill-founded belief that neo-classical economic theory had no useful application in Third World countries.

'This fallacy, which he calls the "dirigiste dogma", rests primarily upon the idea that, if economic development is to be promoted, the price mechanism or the market economy needs to be supplanted ... by direct government controls. ...

'The inconvenient fact that almost all people, including the most impoverished peasants, given the opportunity, do act "economically", do create markets, do apply real prices to goods and services, runs directly against the dirigiste dogma. With appalling consequences, Third World politicians have preferred the pseudo-scientific judgements of Western academics to the evidence of their own eyes.'   Matthew Symonds, *Daily Telegraph*

'... a *tour d'horizon* ... one of the most concise and cogent rejections of "development economics".'   Michael Prest, *The Times*

'Mr Deepak Lal strongly criticises the "dirigiste dogma" which has dominated policy towards developing countries. He says this dogma has encouraged countries to turn inwards and foster a hot-house, import-substituting industrialisation behind high protective walls when the real gains have been had by countries such as South Korea which have lowered tariffs.'

David Tonge, *Financial Times*

'... shows full familiarity with the literature and his book will be useful to all those interested in development economics, whether they agree with his criticism or not.'

H. W. Singer, *British Book News*

Hobart Paper 97
THE PRICE OF STABILITY ...?
A study of price fluctuations in primary products with alternative proposals for stabilisation
Sir Sydney Caine   1983   £1·50

'. . . a new Hobart Paper by Sir Sydney Caine has some realistic analysis to offer. The paper points out that commodity price volatility tends to be endemic because crops are unpredictable; the elasticities of both supply and demand are low; and the industrialised countries limit access to their markets by support systems for their own producers, so that the impact of fluctuations in supply and demand is concentrated on a narrower free market.

'. . . As befits a paper from the IEA, the proposed solutions place emphasis on improving the market mechanism. . . . [it] recommends the development of long-term contractual purchasing arrangements, whereby an international agency would act as a broker in arranging contracts for longer periods than are available through existing exchanges. . . . Such a scheme would certainly reduce uncertainty. The question is whether any commercial agent would provide guarantees and whether the scheme could operate without them.'   *Financial Times*, in an Editorial

Hobart Paper 94
WILL CHINA GO 'CAPITALIST'?
An economic analysis of property rights and institutional change
Steven N. S. Cheung   1982   £1·50

Professor of Economics at the University of Hong Kong, Cheung draws on his deep understanding of the historical roots of Chinese society and predicts that the country is on 'the road to capitalism'. Because of the current 'open door policies', Cheung contends that China will eventually adopt a structure of property rights similar to Hong Kong and Japan.

Hobart Paper 81
HOW JAPAN COMPETES: A VERDICT ON 'DUMPING'
An assessment of international trading practices with special reference to 'dumping'
G. C. Allen *With a Commentary by* **Yukihide Okano**
1978   £1·50

Hobart Paper 55
MACROMANCY
The ideology of 'development economics'
Douglas Rimmer 1973 50p
'Strongly recommended for teachers' reading and suitable for the better "A" Level pupil.'
Economics, Journal of the Economics Association

Research Monograph 27
INDIA: PROGRESS OR POVERTY?
A review of the outcome of central planning in India, 1951-69
Sudha Shenoy 1971 £1·00
'The number of publications on India issued in foreign countries is legion, but they are mostly marred by bias or passion. Miss Shenoy avoids both and writes dispassionately to give her readers a critical evaluation of India's five year plans.' *Hindusthan Standard*

Occasional Paper 22
CHOICE: LESSONS FROM THE THIRD WORLD
Peter du Sautoy 1968 50p
'Peter du Sautoy . . . was a government official in Ghana for many years before becoming Lecturer in Community Development at Manchester University. . . . He points out that while grasping the material benefits the West has to offer, the developing countries are by no means anxious to absorb our social attitudes and accept them as superior to their own. Perhaps, as Mr du Sautoy says, we need "a more childlike mind" to survive in a democratic society.' *Director*

Research Monograph 6
JOHN STUART MILL'S OTHER ISLAND
A study of the economic development of Hong Kong
Henry Smith 1966 50p
'Mr Henry Smith, vice-principal of Ruskin College, Oxford . . . explains the unusual title he has chosen for this study as a compliment to the classical economist's belief in private enterprise qualified by public ownership of land. He thinks that Hong Kong is a good example of such a situation [and] makes the point that since Hong Kong enjoys complete free trade and imports much food, for many consumers' goods and the bulk of materials from which the consumers' goods are made, world prices rule and the trend is set by forces outside the colony. . . . Yet, with absolute freedom and the minimum of State direction in economic matters the level of economic production in the colony has expanded sufficiently to outstrip the growth of population.' *Glasgow Herald*